May y[...]
As your Lord & Savior

From

RANGE RIDIN'

to

SOUL SEEKIN'

PASTOR JAMES SCOTT
WYOMING COWBOY PREACHER

outskirts
press

Dedication

Writing a book has been on the front of my mind for at least the past five or six years. I would often tell my wife that I should write a book someday about this or about that. She would always graciously say, "that would be a great idea." So, Rebecca, I want you to know that your inspirations have finally led to something beyond me just thinking about writing. When you read this for the very first time, it means that this book will have been published for you and the whole world to read and, hopefully, enjoy. My love, you have inspired me since the day we got saved, to become more and more like Christ each day. I thank you from the bottom of my heart and until the day I die, you will always be my lifetime wife.

I would also like to thank so many friends who have encouraged me along the way to always go above and beyond and keep pushing until this book was finished. Your words have challenged me and given me more courage to step up and become a voice for the Gospel even when it was tough and challenging. Words cannot adequately express how much you all mean to me. I truly value your friendships and all of the insights you have been willing to share.

Finally, Lord I thank you for saving a soul like mine. You reached down and pulled me out of the darkness where I used to live. Your love, mercy and grace now abound in my life. I am humbled beyond words! This book would never have been possible without You saving my life and guiding my thoughts. I pledge that for the rest of my days, I will tell the world about Your goodness and Your grace. I love you, Lord, with all of my heart, soul, mind and strength. God, please take this work and make it into something far greater than just words on pages written by James Scott. And, may you receive all the honor and glory!

James Scott

Foreword

I could choose to introduce this book to you or I could choose to introduce the author, James Scott. I would like to do a little of both. Although, I believe that shedding light on either will say plenty about the other also.

James is a brand-new author. This is his very first book and I was honored to get a sneak peek at the manuscript. I know James very well. I have seen him in action on the front lines of ministry and evangelism. I have heard him preach. I have watched him teach. I have personally seen him lead people to faith in Jesus Christ. It is abundantly clear that God has called, equipped and set James apart for the unique, kingdom-building work that he does every day. Also, I have already read the pages that you are about to read. So, without reservation, I can proudly recommend to you both the author and the book.

James managed to cast a very wide net with this book. It is part auto-biography, part evangelism training 101, part Bible instruction, and part inspiration, and part storytelling as only a cowboy preacher from Wyoming can do. It is partly for the unchurched. It is partly for new Christians. It is partly for seasoned believers. But above all, it is a blueprint for how to become a passionate follower of the Lord Jesus Christ and serve Him effectively in the real world. And yes, in case you were wondering, certain chapters serve as a swift kick in the pants for any Christians who like to *talk* about their faith more than they like to *live* out their faith before God and others.

There are at least two main things that make this book unique and a must-read for every Christian on the planet. First, James did not sit in an ivory tower and dream up hypothetical scenarios to write about. In fact, it is sometimes a humorous image to even try to picture James in an office. You are much more likely to find him on a horse and you are much, much, much more likely to find him engaging in one-on-one or one-on-two gospel conversations with people on the street. Far from a detached, theoretical, or "scholarly" perspective, James uses his first-hand experience of many years on the front lines of the spiritual battlefield to help other believers become potent servants of God. Of course, there is nothing the matter with a so-called scholarly approach to writing. But there are already plenty of those books on the market. We need more, not fewer, books written by the people who have been there and done that.

The second main thing that makes this book stand out is related to the first. Because James is an authentic cowboy (true statement!), and he is not trying to compose a Ph.D. dissertation, his writing voice is simple and honest. The book will MORE than make you think, but it is written in a way that is easy to understand. It could be said like this: James, in plain ole English, is going to tell you about how God saved him, how God uses him to advance the Kingdom, and how YOU too, can be used by God in a powerful way to make a difference in people's lives. Oh, and if you do not yet know the Lord, James is not going to beat you up for it. But he is also not going to pull any punches on what sort of eternity awaits folks who won't accept Christ into their lives as Savior and Lord.

I enjoyed this book very much. I laughed. I cried. I felt spiritually convicted on more than one occasion. You are going to enjoy it too, and I believe this book will benefit every Christian everywhere. I know I speak for James when I say, To God be the Glory!

Shane Stone, Ph.D.
Assoc. Professor, Colorado Christian University

Table of Contents

Introduction

I KNOW WHAT you are thinking; "here's another book I'm never going to read." Maybe that is a true statement. But what if I could convince you otherwise? I have attempted to write this book in such a way that it will reach and assist people who typically do not read very many books. By the way, I am highly qualified to write such a book, because I was exactly that person for most of my life. Listen, when I was in school, I was the one who would have girls write book reports for me. So, yes, I totally understand your skepticism. But this book is different. Trust me!

I grew up hating the idea that somebody was making me take time out of my life to read and study. From junior high all the way through high school, I spent *a lot* of time letting (or should I say persuading?) others to help me get through whatever assignment I was tasked with. I found out later in life, that did far more harm than good. In fact, it became obvious that

I had cheated myself in many ways. The older I get, I am more and more convinced about the old saying, "knowledge is power." The more knowledge I have, the better I can effectively communicate with people, or just chime in on a conversation. And as I began walking closer and closer with Jesus, it turns out that I actually had important things to say!

I have also come to realize that a good many of the books out there are written by people with a lot of letters behind their names: Ph.D., D.Min., M.Div., M.D., ABC or ZYX. My name is Pastor James Scott, period. I'm pleased to meet you! I am just an ordinary man who felt compelled to write this book. In fact, I believe I am in great company. Jesus Christ himself picked 12 VERY ordinary men to help lead and change the world. There were no fancy letters behind any of their names. Let's put to rest the myth that people without letters behind their names aren't allowed to do big things. If God has laid something on our hearts, then you and I are just as qualified as Dr. So-and-So to say it out loud. In fact, we have no choice BUT to speak, write, sing, shout, or whatever it takes to give God glory. We can all do this, and that is exactly what I am trying to do— put into words the things God has laid on my heart.

You see, I don't get my strength from a title behind my name. I get my strength from Christ. The Bible gives us a great reminder of this; "I can do all this through him (Christ) who gives me strength" (Philippians 4:13, NIV). So, as you begin to read this book, just know that the author is merely being himself. I am not a "know-it-all," but I am also not afraid to step out of my comfort zone and write this book. I am strengthened by the Lord Jesus Christ. My prayer is that this book will not only encourage you but also challenge you. God wants you to do the very best with what you have been given, but He promises to give you the strength to do so. God does not show favoritism (Romans 2:11, NIV) and so you and I are on the same playing field. The only difference is you could possibly be the one holding yourself back. I can say that too, because that is who I once was. I missed out on many opportunities and blessings from the Lord, because I just assumed that I was less than who I was supposed to be. Praise God I no longer think like that. God in His almighty holiness has changed the way I think about everything in this life, including how I view my personal role in the Kingdom.

If this stubborn cowboy from Wyoming can have his mind changed, then there is also hope for all who read this book. We are perfectly capable of learning new things. We do not have to "stay in our lane." We are trainable, but we must first acknowledge that there is a lot more out there than what we currently know (and do). "There is more than one way to skin a cat" is an old adage that comes to mind. Be thinking that way while reading this book. My ways of reaching people with the Gospel are not the only ways by any means. They are, however, tried and true and will work for most anybody who is willing to put in the effort. If you want to be godlier and become a deeper Christian, then YOU are the audience I am trying to reach. If you want to learn to share your faith anytime and anywhere, I am here to help you. Grab you a cup of coffee or a nice hot tea and enjoy what God has laid on my heart to share. My whole purpose is to inspire others to be *even* more faithful and obedient to Him.

A 300-inch class 6x6 bull elk.

CHAPTER **1**

The Call

AS A YOUNG boy, I grew up loving to hunt and fish and be outdoors at any given time. Even when I got married and started having children, those outdoor drives were still there. In the summer of 2000, I remember reading an article in Field and Stream magazine. It said instead of walking up to a property owner's door and asking them for permission to hunt, try this technique instead. Walk up and introduce yourself to the land owner. Explain why you are there and in return for being allowed to hunt or fish on their lands, that you would be more than glad to work some on their place to help them out. It was kind of like giving something back instead of just taking something from them. I thought to myself, "Wow! I should try that." That fall, I had a trophy buck deer tag in the state of Wyoming. I found a ranch that I wanted to hunt. I took the time to do just what that article had said. Guess what? It worked. The lady I spoke with said that she would be more than willing to allow me to hunt in exchange for helping her on the ranch. It truly was a win-win situation.

Now, I had been pretty much raised in a small town up until that point. My wife and I would bring our children out to this ranch and we were able to expose them to a whole new culture. Meanwhile, I was absolutely falling in love with the whole ranching idea. It was work like I had never done before. We were riding horses, irrigating hay fields, fixing fence, building fence, roping calves, fixing machinery, and everything else that went into the ranching lifestyle. My wife was enjoying it just as much as I was.

In the first six months of working for hunting privileges, my wife and I bought our very first set of cows. We bought 12 pairs and the momma cows were bred back. We were in the cattle business! We then started buying some horses. I had learned how to break horses from an older man named Nate Brown. He was in his late 70's at that time. He was a great teacher and I was learning everything possible that went along with being a *real* rancher. So, thus began our ranching career in the year 2000. What does that have to do with reaching lost souls for Christ? Well, it was a "God thing." For 10 years we worked and helped to manage, or all together managed ranches for other people. We would later lease our own ranch in order to continue to raise our three boys in that lifestyle.

In the heart of ranch country, in the middle of nowhere Montana, is where I first experienced God impressing upon my heart and soul these next few words: "There are people who you know and don't know, James, who are dying and going to hell. What are you doing about it?" I have to believe that the majority of people, if completely honest with themselves, would be forced to say "nothing—that's what I'm doing about it." And that was my answer too. Lord, I am doing nothing about people dying and going to hell. It was not fun to confess, but it was the truth. So, in 2009, while riding the range in eastern Montana, just my horse, dogs, and me, God confronted me with that question. His question, and my truthful but feeble answer served as a major turning point in my life.

I was saved back in 2001 but had not really lived much of a Christlike life until God spoke to my heart that penetrating question. I somehow thought that when I got saved, that was it. I was going to heaven and that was all I really needed to know. Little did I realize those first several years of my Christian walk, that getting "saved" meant a whole lot more. I have thought about this for many years. Why not just get saved and die and go to heaven? I mean, after all, that's where the good stuff is, right? For most people that is not when the end of life occurs. God tends to leave us around, often for many decades, AFTER we get saved.

With that in mind, I have come to realize that God saves us and <u>then</u> reveals HIS purpose for the remainder of OUR lives. You heard correctly. God has a purpose for each and every single one of us. He foreknew you even before you existed. Jeremiah 1:5 says, "Before I formed you in the womb I knew you, before you were born I set you apart..." (NIV). Now, in context, this was about appointing Jeremiah as a prophet. But, if God knew the prophet Jeremiah, then my friend He knew you too. There is no escaping this truth. Well before we were born, God knew us and set us apart from the world. Your destination is heaven, but you probably have much work to do before you arrive there.

Can you think back to who shared the Word of God with you in a way that made you realize that you needed a Savior and that Savior's name was Jesus Christ? Somebody did that for you. The old saying that "the buck stops here" should <u>not</u> be applied to us when we hear the Gospel. If the Gospel stopped at you, how sad of a day that would be. If you never shared the

Gospel, how then do others hear about the only way to heaven?

That day on the ranch has forever changed my own life; after all, here I am sharing these thoughts with you now. But I got home from riding that day with a very heavy heart. I knew that I had an encounter with God like maybe I had never had before. I realized that He was seeking to get my attention. God was speaking to me in a way that I could understand Him. I had two choices. I could either keep on riding and living my life exactly the same, or I could listen to the One who was tugging at my heart.

I went home and told my wife about the experience I had. As a good wife would, she said "you had better pray over this." I prayed and prayed and God continued to make Himself known to me. My life was great at the time. I was not looking to change a thing. I could ride horses all day long. I could throw my rope on anything I thought I was tough enough to catch. I had three wonderful children and a beautiful, caring, and loving wife. Now as a side note, those are not in order. My wife is at the top of that list. But as I started to examine my personal life, I asked myself, "What am I doing to further the kingdom of God?" And again, that dog-gone word "nothing" came to my mind. I knew I needed to change that.

I had read at some point that I was saved for a purpose. I needed to seek and find out what my purpose was. I was a cowboy, not a preacher or a speaker. Most cowboys I know are not comfortable speaking in front of many people. I told God that if He could use a cowboy like me, then I would surrender to whatever He was calling or asking me to do. The key word there is "calling." Being a pastor is not a job. You can't just wake up tomorrow and think you will change careers. Throughout the whole entire Bible, there is not one case recorded of somebody being in the ministry and then deciding to move onto something else. When God calls you, it is because He has a specific purpose in mind, and He equips you for your calling.

After being in the ministry for over 10 years, I sometimes wonder who in their right mind would *want* to be a pastor, evangelist, or a ministry leader? There is nothing easy about it. But anything that is easy is usually not worth doing; at least that is the old saying. To be perfectly honest, I wouldn't trade it for anything. I get to see and do things that most people never get to see or experience.

So again, I say ministry is a *calling* not a job or a career choice. God calls you into the ministry. I thought about the prophet Isaiah. He heard the voice of God saying, "Whom shall I send? And who will go for us"

(Isaiah 6:8a, NIV)? And he responded, "Here am I. Send me" (Isaiah 6:8b, NIV). I realized at that moment I was being called to share the saving grace of Jesus Christ with other people. I had been saved for a reason and a purpose. That purpose was to point and lead others to Jesus. The whole point of my life was finally being revealed to me. I was both excited and nervous at the same time. Could God really use somebody as finite as me? I kept going back to God asking Him that same question again and again. God, can you really use somebody like me? But then I remembered that Jesus started out with 12 ordinary, mostly uneducated men. I fit that ticket loud and clear! My friend you can fit this ticket as well.

Like Isaiah, I had what God already had put inside of me. I was at the point of my life where I wanted to be obedient to His calling. It wasn't the educated or uneducated that Christ was so concerned with. It wasn't age or experience. He was much more interested in my obedience to follow Him when He says, "Come follow me" (Matthew 4:19, 19:21; Mark 1:17, 10:21; & Luke 18:22, NIV). That official call of God was put on my life in 2009 to share Christ. It would have been great if I would have just said, "Okay Lord I am all yours and I am all in." But you guessed it, I didn't.

I moved onto one more ranch in North Dakota. I ranched full-time and preached every other Sunday at a little Baptist church on an Indian reservation. God had called me, but I did not answer Him fully. My life seemed very unsettled. Although I was preaching some and studying in the Word, things were not as they should have been, and deep down I knew it. A mentor from another town came into my life. He shared with me that God had a plan and a purpose for all of His people. He told me that if we were not in God's will, our lives would often seem and sometimes look upside down. Without him knowing my situation, he was telling me everything that was already going on in my life.

Again, I shared this with my wife and again she said "Babe you better pray and listen to what God is asking you to do." Finally, God was breaking through my thick skull. I made a couple of phone calls back to my home state of Wyoming and told a few friends that I felt that God was calling me into the ministry as a church planter. One of them said "I knew that a long time ago."

I kept on praying on how to leave the ranch job and start what was going to be one of the scariest and most adventurous times of my life. As I was lying in bed one night, I told God that I was going to fast until noon the next day. I would not recommend giving God a time frame like that, but that is what I did. I woke up in the morning very hungry, as usual. I went out and did my chores and came back in around 11:00 a.m. My wife was aware of the "deadline" I had given the God of the universe! Again, don't do that, but that is what I did. At that time, the phone rang and it was my boss. He was an older man who was very set in his ways. He called to inform me that he was going to sell the cows and lease out the ranch. The bottom line was that he didn't need me anymore as his ranch foreman. I hung up the phone and shared this with my wife. She said well what do you think God is trying to tell you? Like most stubborn men, I said "I don't know." She said, "Babe, God is clearing the way for you to go and accept the calling on your life." As I sat down and really pondered what was happening, it was obvious that things were starting to align the way that God had planned all along. He was in control and had set in motion a chain of events even before I had a clue that I would grow someday to serve Him in any sort of ministry capacity.

**Where our first ministry began;
under a tree in Hyattville Wyoming.**

CHAPTER 2

Answering the Call

WHEN YOUR CAREER changes, everything changes in your life. We moved back to Worland, Wyoming and lived with my sister-in-law until we found a small ranch to lease outside of Manderson, Wyoming. We went to work right away with the plans that God was laying on my heart. We began our ministry in a campground near Hyattville, Wyoming. We would hold Sunday morning church services under a tree where campers and locals could meet and worship together. We also began a Thursday evening Bible study in different peoples' homes. We were learning as we were ministering.

In small-town Wyoming there is not a church on every corner. In fact, to try and find like-minded believers was a challenge in itself. What we found, though, was that the people who *did* believe like us were quite encouraged to have studies brought so close to where they lived. We were growing in numbers, but more importantly we were all growing in the Word of God. I came to realize that *some* people were flat-out hungry for the Word. I also noticed that outside of our little group of believers was a world full of lost souls who couldn't care less that someone was teaching or preaching about Jesus. I discovered that not everybody (in fact, not very many people at all) actually believed what I believed. Getting into ministry opened my eyes to a sobering realization. Most people that I encountered on a daily basis didn't seem to be even remotely interested in learning about Jesus or even how to be saved.

One of my first negative conversations was in a café. Somebody asked me what I was doing there. I shared with them that God had called me into the ministry to share Him with the people in and around Hyattville. This person said to me, "we already have a church here, we don't need another one." This statement came from somebody who attended that church. I thought to myself, why would anybody say something like that? I was not there to steal or take away people from an already existing church. I felt that God was asking me to find people who were not saved and not going to church.

I was shocked that a "Christian" would say something like that to me. Not long of being in the ministry I found out something that made me very sad. Just because somebody <u>says</u> they are a Christian does not necessarily make them a Christian. In the cowboy world we say it like this: *If you have to tell somebody that you are a cowboy, then you probably ain't one.* Does that make sense? If I were a mechanic, my mechanic skills should tell people that I am a mechanic. But if I never spent time in a garage fixing cars or trucks, then I better not tell people that I am a mechanic. Your actions should speak louder than your words.

In Matthew 7:21 Jesus says "Not everyone who says to me, 'Lord, Lord,' will enter the kingdom of heaven, but only the one who does the will of my Father who is in heaven" (NIV). I had read that verse plenty of times before, but I had never made the connection that some who say they are a Christian are really not a Christian at all. Sometimes a wolf dresses up in lamb's clothing. The Bible teaches that they will know we are a Christian by our love (John 13:35). At that point in the day, I did not see nor feel any love.

The good news, however, was that the call on my life was bigger than ever and certainly outweighed the fact that somebody didn't want me to be ministering in their community. Hence, the small cowboy church service in the campground was started and a Bible Study on Thursday nights commenced. The ministry that God called us into was well underway in small-town Wyoming.

CHAPTER **3**

Faith or Faithless

IN RURAL AND small-town Wyoming, a person can really only "plant churches" for so many hours in the day. To be honest, people will get tired of you. So, it wasn't too long until I believed that God was opening up doors outside of just planting a church. I agree that when you are called into the ministry you do have certain types of people that you minister to. At the same time, though, lost people and hurting people are in fact just that; lost and hurting. They are everywhere and don't always make it onto the local church's radar screen.

I had driven by this certain building countless times near Basin, Wyoming. One day I read the sign and it said it was a retirement center. God laid it on my heart to go and minister to those who were there. I thought, "God this is crazy. I don't even know one person there." I was new to the ministry and was determined to be faithful and obedient to God, so I looked up the phone number and I called. I got a recorded voice saying push one for this, two for that and so on. I pushed number four. I can tell you that God was in the middle of this. The director of the center answered the call. I sheepishly introduced myself and told her that I believed that God wanted me to come and be a witness to their residents. To my surprise the lady said, "This is wonderful! I have been praying for somebody to come and minster here to them." We set up a time and a day and the rest of that was history. I got off the phone and realized that God had an amazing command of the timing and direction on my life.

God had taken control of my life and He was leading me step by step. Proverbs 16:9 says, "In their hearts humans plan their course, but the Lord establishes their steps" (NIV). I knew in my heart that I wanted to serve God. I just didn't always know exactly what He was asking me to do. So, the God of the universe looked down on His servant and determined my steps. He was leading me by the hand. I was letting go of my human hopes, dreams and fears and instead began letting God be God in every aspect of my life. I was finally allowing God to give me new hopes and new dreams (hint: anything from God is always better than what we can dream up for ourselves). It seemed that I was finally living for the Lord instead of living for just myself.

At that point, the direction in my life was two-fold. I was being a witness to those who were Christians (but merely living out the rest of their days here on earth) AND to those who still had not called on Jesus. As a pastor or minister or lay person, we need to be aware of both types of people in our lives. I believe it is safe to say that there are two types of people – saved and not saved yet (and even some of the saved are not fully surrendered to God). Each day we need to minister to both types. There are only two places that we can spend our eternity, so that must mean that there are only two groups of people.

How do we minister to the saved? We encourage, empower, show empathy, and love them:

Encourage: We need to encourage our saved people to share their faith stories with the lost. Our faith story, much of the time, will resonate with the person with whom we are sharing. I can't tell you how many times I have shared my faith story with an unbeliever about how my marriage was on the rocks and the person looking back at me was going through the very same ordeal. I also have seen Christians who have a personal story of overcoming alcoholism or drug addiction just

FROM RANGE RIDIN' TO SOUL SEEKIN'

happen to be sharing with a person who is struggling with the exact same problem. Coincidence? I think not. I believe God scheduled a divine appointment between the ones sharing their faith story and the ones listening. That is how God can work. Our stories will encourage other people and will also give them hope to get through their struggle.

As saved people, many of us have fought our own demons. By the grace of God, we have overcome them. Not on our own accord, but because of Jesus's intervention in our lives. You and I are <u>not</u> strong enough to take on and overcome the evils of this world by ourselves. Jesus said, "I have told you these things, so that in me you may have peace. In this world you will have trouble. But take heart! I have overcome the world" (John 16:33, NIV). Man, that makes my heart leap for joy. It's not *if* we are going to have trouble, but *when* we have it. It's not *if* Jesus can help us out, it's He has *already* overcome it if we would let Him into our lives, eternally, but also day in and day out.

Sometimes we must encourage our saved friends when they get discouraged. Remind them that God is not only the God on the mountain, but is also God in the valley in our lives. If we ever feel lonely or abandoned, we should remember that God is not the one who leaves us. You and I are the ones who leave God.

We tend to put God on the back burner sometimes. God is always there just waiting for us to come back to Him. That, my friends, is what love looks like. If we could get to that point in our lives, we would have all the encouragement we need PLUS it would overflow from us like a river and have a powerful effect on others. It sounds like what the Psalmist means when he says that his "cup overflows" (Psalm 23:5b, NIV). When our cup overflows, I think it is important to make sure that it runs onto somebody else. It just makes sense. Let us not keep it to ourselves.; we need to be a blessing to somebody else along the way.

Empower: Strength and confidence seem to be words associated with the idea of empowerment. If we were to examine the typical American Christian today what would we find? I hope you will continue to read this book, because from here on out, it's going to get a little messy. My prayer has always been to not step on anybody's *toes*, but that God would use my spoken or written words to pierce somebody's *heart*. That is what we need (by the way, I need that too!). Our toes are not what matter the most. On the other hand, our hearts are sensitive and often fragile, but that is what God cares about far more. But if you cut to the chase of the *heart* of the matter, then and only then can we see where changes in our lives need to be made.

Christians need that heart-jolting message on a regular basis. They go to church one or maybe even two times a week. Some even make it to Sunday school. For a large part of my life I never made that a very high priority. Why? Because I didn't fully realize what it was about. I now know that it is the Sunday teaching part of the day. It is where we learn some of the Bible stories as well as learn to somehow apply what we learned that day in real life. Sunday school is for teaching and Sunday "church" is for preaching. So, they teach us and they preach at us. What's the difference? When they teach us, we should be learning this knowledge and be able to store it up for when we need it. When they preach to us, we should take to heart what they are preaching about. A good sermon should not only hit us in our hearts but should convict us enough to use it as fuel for the week as we go out into battle in the world for lost souls (This is why "soul seekin'" is part of the title of this book).

How long does your truck run without putting any diesel or gas in it? If you drive it a lot, then not very long. It is the same reasoning with us as we share our faith. If you don't share the knowledge that you have about Jesus and how to get to heaven, your tank stays pretty full. I might also add that a full tank all of the time can and will become very stagnant. This is a place that none of us want to be, but where a lot of us are. But if you are out there day after day sharing and trying to lead others to Christ, your tank gets empty fairly quickly. You must fill up your spiritual gas tank often. Good sermons (and books) will do that for you.

So, if you think it is not all that important to share your faith with others, but you continue to attend church services and Sunday school, one might wonder what the whole point is. I am pretty well convinced that God is not looking for Sunday morning Christians. I promise you that nobody will win an award for being the best church pew warmer when we get to heaven. In fact, that phrase, "Sunday morning Christian," should not even exist. How can one be a Christian one day of the week? There's no such thing. You are either a Christian or not. If you are a Christian then you should be sold out to Jesus seven days per week, not one.

When you realize that every person who crosses your path has a soul and that soul is headed to one place or another, then we know as Christians that we simply must share with that person the only way to heaven (Jesus Christ). These are things we should all be doing but are not doing on nearly a large enough scale. I have read somewhere in the past that perhaps only about two-percent of evangelical Christians share their faith. That my friends, is a totally inexcusable number. What must God think about such a tiny percentage of those He has already saved refusing to share His love with others? Hint: He probably doesn't think very highly of it!

My friend, ask yourself this question. How sold out to Jesus Christ are you? Some might say 50% or 60% or 75% or maybe even 98%. Wow, 98% *sounds* pretty dog-gone good, right? Now let me pick on the husbands for a minute. Husbands, you come home from working all day and your beautiful wife has a five-course meal waiting for you on the table. There are candles lit and roses all around. Your beautiful and lovely wife comes up to you and puts her arms around your shoulders, looks you smack dab in the eyes and says, "honey I just want you to know that I am 98% committed and faithful to you and to you alone." How in the world are you going to react? Well, no peaceful and relaxing supper now (Lol). This is not good at all, right? Not one man alive is going to be okay with his wife being 98% faithful to him. Why? Because we require our wives to be 100% faithful to us, and they require the same thing in return.

Can I ask this question? Husband, can your wife save you? The answer is absolutely not. Not at all. If we expect our spouses to be 100% faithful to us, then why do we think that we can be anything less than 100% faithful to God who actually *can* save us? He doesn't want to be our God part-time or even just when we think we need Him. God wants to be the biggest and most important part of your life all of the time, not just part of the time. Anything less than being 100% sold out to Jesus Christ is simply not good enough. Christians, we need to empower other believers to get to this point in their life. Anything less than 100% commitment is simply not desirable.

As mature Christians we can be helping new believers and struggling believers to become sold-out to Jesus Christ. My friend, I told you earlier I was not trying for your toes, but for your heart. When we realize that we can always give more of ourselves because of how much Christ means to us, it should hit us in our heart. It should make us realize how much more there is to do and that WE are the ones who need to be doing it. If Jesus Christ means the world to us, then why not tell the world what Jesus Christ can do for them? When we empower others with the truth we can and will build their confidence in such a way that we will start to see a change in the average Christian and in their walk with Jesus.

Empathy: More or less, this is the ability to understand and share the feelings of another. Every person reading this book should have empathy in their lives. As a saved person, I can relate to a lost person. Why? Because at one point, I was lost and dying and going to hell, exactly the same as them. Saved people don't get saved; lost people get saved. Saved people don't need salvation, but they certainly need to be growing stronger, and more obedient and faithful.

When witnessing to people about Jesus, you must put yourself in their lost shoes. This is not hard to do at all. Some of us have spent more time on this earth lost than saved. You can be empathetic toward them. Explain to the lost person who you were before you got saved. Then share with them why *they* need to be saved. Share with them who God is and what God has done in your life. If the conversation is still flowing, then ask them if they would like to get saved *right now*. Ask them if they are ready to receive God's ultimate grace and mercy *today*.

When preaching, I never give the Gospel without an invitation for people to respond by placing faith in Christ. And here is the main reason why: The great evangelist D.L. Moody learned this lesson the painful way. It has long been repeated that he had one great regret in his life. On October 8, 1871, he was leading a revival in Chicago. He preached his heart out and clearly communicated the Gospel. When he was done preaching, he simply told the people to go home and see if they thought they needed the forgiveness of Christ Jesus. He basically said, if you think you need Him, then come back tomorrow and we will do business with God. He then dismissed the crowd. That night was the beginning of the Great Chicago Fires that decimated the city. The next evening, he realized that some of the ones who were there the night before never made it out alive from the fires. He was devastated. He knew that these people needed to make a decision to follow Christ but did not give them the opportunity right then and right there on the previous evening. He chose to wait a day so that they could think about it. His choice haunted him for the rest of his life. He went on to say that it was his gravest regret. Many preachers have learned from Moody. Most evangelists, if not all, never give people until the next day to make a decision. Why? Because what if they don't get tomorrow to make the most important decision they will ever make? That is why when you present the Gospel, whether it be to 1 or 1001, you should always give the opportunity for Christ to be accepted and for sins to be forgiven.

There have been times in my own life when I have shared with people about God, but not given them the opportunity to accept the greatest gift given to mankind.

Regretfully, I can say that some of those people are no longer here today. I have failed many times in properly sharing the Gospel and then challenging people to make a decision before it's too late. When we fail, though, we need to learn from our failures. If we truly never learn, then we might have to start asking ourselves if we are even in it for the right reasons. The story is often repeated about the hall of fame basketball player, Michael Jordan, suggesting that he had *missed* more than 9,000 shots in his career. He then said that he had *lost* nearly 300 games. At least 26 times, he said he was entrusted to take the game-winning shot and *missed*. He admitted that he had *failed* over and over and over again in his life, but then proposed that those failures were the whole reason for his incredible successes.

Don't be afraid to fail, but strive to actually learn from your mistakes. Learn what *not* to do so you will know what *to do*. When you figure this out in your life, your failures will begin to turn into successes. I once had a boss named Tim Amdahl who told me how he would do something. Then he would say the reason he knew that was because he had tried numerous ways before that didn't work. Never let failure be the last thing you experience, but let it play a part in shaping you into who you are meant to be.

Your realization that a person may not be in heaven simply because you did not share Christ with them, should make you want to be much more effective at sharing the Gospel. Now when given the opportunity, I make a full-fledged, conscious effort to share the Gospel and to give that person a chance to respond to the Good News.

Bob Smiley is a Christian comedian. I recall a great story he referred to as the hot tub story. He got done with a show one day and headed up to the hotel's pool room to relax by himself in the hot tub. As he was soaking, he heard the door open. He turned around and there stood the biggest and hairiest man he had ever seen. The man walked up to the hot tub and cannon-balled in. Bob was trying with finesse to get out of the tub. He made it halfway out, and the man said, "mister can I ask you something?" Bob turned around and said, "yeah, what is it?" The man said "do you know who Jesus Christ is?" Bob sank back into the tub and said "yes I do; He is my Lord and Savior. I actually travel the country and tell people about His love and mercy." The man said, "well that is great. I just didn't want to miss an opportunity to tell somebody about the greatness of our God." Bob went on to say that he realized that man had taught him a very important lesson.

You see, how powerful would it be if we would wake up each morning and simply ask God to give us an encounter with somebody who does not know Jesus? We normally will not know anything about the spiritual condition of the other person unless you are bold enough to simply ask the question. As Christians, it should not be that hard to simply say to someone, "hey, do you know who Jesus Christ is?" How they respond will dictate where the conversation goes from there (It may go nowhere, or it may be life-changing for that person). Remember, if you are saved, you too were lost at one point. Empathize with them, love them, care for them, and reach out to them. And most importantly, share with them the greatest story ever told to mankind – the greatest love story ever told, period, the Gospel of Jesus Christ.

When you set out to share your faith, things are going to happen; good things and bad things. First off, the devil does not want you to share your faith with one single lost soul. He is there to fill your head with all sorts of lies and misconceptions. In fact, he is a liar and the father of lies (John 8:44b, NIV). Don't believe what he is trying to say to you or impress upon you. The devil will try his best to stop you from doing what you set out to do. But once we are aware that he

ALWAYS tries to interfere when we share the Gospel, we can be prepared.

The Lord tells us to not be afraid. In fact, some variation of that phrase appears roughly 365 times in the Bible. Guess what? Maybe we should heed that advice. After all, what do we have to be afraid of? Rejection? My friend, that other person is not rejecting you or I, they are (and have been) rejecting the Redeemer of the world and the Redeemer of their soul. You and I are simply acting like the hands and feet of Christ while we are here in this world. We are His humble servants – His vessels to work through. When they knock you down with their words, dust yourself off and move along to the next conversation.

Many times, I have shared with people who did not believe that there was a God. When I ask them if they would like to accept Christ and give their life to Him, their response is typically something like, "I am not interested." I have learned to say this back to them: "My prayer for you is that God will give you enough time for somebody else to come into your life so that they may share with you again how real this Jesus really is." Some have actually thanked me for that. When this happens, it means it simply wasn't their time to come to faith in Christ. There is no reason whatsoever to feel offended or rejected.

The Bible says, "No man can come to me, except the Father which hath sent me draw him: and I will raise him up at the last day" (John 6:44, KJV). So, every person has to be drawn to God in order for that person to become saved. I have found this to be true time and time again. When it's not their time, it cannot and will not happen. You and I are not able to force God's hand. But when it *is* their time, it doesn't matter when or where, because you and I couldn't stop it even if we wanted to. The Holy Spirit convicts us of our sin in our lives and moves us to repentance and acceptance of His saving grace. It is a most treasured moment to watch somebody right in front of your eyes to be transformed by the power of the Holy Spirit.

I first saw this back in Sturgis, South Dakota many years ago. I was there to share my "three-minute story" on how Christ changed my life. I was really trying to understand how somebody could get saved in such a short amount of time. Well, God showed me how somebody could be saved. I was sharing my story and the Gospel with this man. He had sunglasses on. As I was sharing, I noticed the tears beginning to well-up behind his glasses and then begin to fall down his cheek. He was so moved by the power of God, that he could hardly even speak a word. He finally managed to pray and receive the greatest gift he had ever been given. It was so powerful. It made me understand that God is God and we are not. We are to do what He asks us to do. He will then do what He is going to do. That my friend is the Power and the Majesty of our God, of our Savior, Jesus Christ.

A Gospel conversation with children in Malawi Africa.

CHAPTER 4

Gospel Sharing Format

IN THIS CHAPTER, I want to share with you the way I teach folks how to share their faith story and the Gospel. This is the format my wife and I often use, especially when presenting the Gospel at special events. Some of this format was originally developed through the North American Mission Board which sought to teach Christians how to evangelize. I modified it, somewhat, several years back. To be honest, I struggled some with the "three-minute story," because to me, it seemed like I found myself speaking too much about myself and did not leave enough time for the Gospel.

***Why* should we share our story**? The Apostle Paul reminds us, "You yourselves are our letter, written on our hearts, known and read by everyone. You show that you are a letter from Christ, the result of our ministry, written not with ink but with the Spirit of the living

God, not on tablets of stone but on tablets of human hearts" (2 Corinthians 3:2-3, NIV). Your life has a story written upon your heart. Good or bad, it is your story. It is your story that has led you to the saving knowledge of JESUS CHRIST. Share it with someone!!!!!

***Where* do we tell our story**? 1 Peter 3:15 says, "But in your hearts revere Christ as Lord. Always be prepared to give an answer to everyone who asks you to give the reason for the hope that you have. But do this with gentleness and respect" (NIV). We should be *ready* at the drop of a hat, and *able* to share our story and the Gospel with anyone who will listen. Do it with gentleness. Be respectful. But do it.

***What* are the benefits of sharing**? "It is written: 'I believed; therefore I have spoken.' Since we have that same spirit of faith, we also believe and therefore speak because we know that the one who raised the Lord Jesus from the dead will also raise us with Jesus and present us with you to himself. All this is for your benefit, so that the grace that is reaching more and more people may cause thanksgiving to overflow to the glory of God" (2 Corinthians 4:13-15, NIV). We will be exceedingly thankful to God that he is a saving God and a God of grace. In fact, the more people that receive God's grace, the more thanks to God we all will give, according to those verses.

What *prohibits* us from sharing? We are too afraid and do not feel adequate enough to openly share. Hebrews 13:20-21 says, "Now may the God of peace, who through the blood of the eternal covenant brought back from the dead our Lord Jesus, that great Shepherd of the sheep, equip you with everything good for doing his will, and may he work in us what is pleasing to him, through Jesus Christ, to whom be glory for ever and ever. Amen" (NIV).

My brother or sister, God will equip you at the right time with the right words to share HIM with someone. The Holy Spirit that lives inside of you because of your salvation is there to guide you and bring you comfort and peace that will transcend your understanding (Philippians 4:7). You are not doing the saving, but only the sharing. God does all of the *saving*!!!!! But He has ordained that YOU do all of the *sharing*.

***How* do you share your story**? We teach the following very simple breakdown. It covers three important aspects of your salvation experience along with the suggested amount of time to spend on each one:

- 45 seconds of what your life was like *before* you knew Jesus.
- 45 seconds of *how* you (personally) got saved and *when*.

35

- 45 seconds of what your life has been like *since* receiving Jesus.

We have found that it is best to write out your story, at least initially. When writing out your story, here are some helpful ideas:

- Do not glorify your sin. Don't make it look like fun. Sin is bad and sin is what keeps us from a perfect God.
- Write out your story using your own words. Don't use churchy words or phrases, such as: Are you covered in the blood? Have you been sanctified? Jesus is our propitiation. Actually, don't even assume that a lost person understands when you say that you were "saved" at a young age. Explain yourself in plain terms.
- Make notecards if you need to in order to practice your presentation.

If you follow the above guidelines, in a three-minute conversation, this will now leave you 45 seconds to share the gospel. What is the Gospel and how can it possibly be shared in 45 seconds? Simple.

Jesus Christ came to this earth and walked it for 33 years. He was nailed to a cross for our sins. He suffered, he died, and he was buried. But three days later,

He rose from the grave. The Bible says "If you declare with your mouth, 'Jesus is Lord,' and believe in your heart that God raised him from the dead, you will be saved. For it is with your heart that you believe and are justified, and it is with your mouth that you profess your faith and are saved" (Romans 10:9-10, NIV). Then verse 13 says "for, Everyone who calls on the name of the Lord will be saved" (NIV). That is a simple Gospel presentation. Jesus came, Jesus died, Jesus arose, and He did this with you in mind. If we would truly believe this in our hearts, and repent of our sins, our eternity will be in Heaven with GOD!

Again, remember there is real value in writing your story out longhand. It is better to write too much and have to trim it down than it is to just start speaking and accidentally leave the most important things out. So, let's give it a try:

What was your life like before Jesus? (45 seconds)
_____
_____
_____
_____
_____
_____

When did you get saved and how? (45 seconds)

_____

_____

_____

_____

_____

_____

What has your life been like since repenting and receiving Jesus? (45 seconds)

_____

_____

_____

_____

_____

_____

Additional helpful tips for thinking through and organizing your story:

- There is an excellent biblical account of faith-sharing. It is very enlightening to read Acts 22 through Acts 26. Paul talks about his former life and how he received Christ and then shares with King Agrippa.
- There are many techniques you can use to share JESUS with someone: Bible verses, the 3-Minute Story, a candy cane, a gospel tract, an evange-cube, a salvation bracelet, the Romans Road. Find one of these ways that you are comfortable

with and learn it frontward and backward. Practice it over and over. YouTube is a great on-line resource to help you learn how to become efficient with any of the above techniques.

- Always remember, the power of God through the Gospel is what will change somebody's life. You and I are only being obedient to God. We get to deliver the Good News and then disciple people once they put their faith in Jesus. But it is God who does the saving.

- There are some 31,102 verses in the Bible. Use the ones that resonate with you. Here are some of my favorites (all taken from the NIV):

John 14:6, "Jesus answered, 'I am the way and the truth and the life. No one comes to the Father except through me.'"

Revelation 3:20, "Here I am! I stand at the door and knock. If anyone hears my voice and opens the door, I will come in and eat with that person, and they with me."

Proverbs 11:30, "The fruit of the righteous is a tree of life, and the one who is wise saves lives."

Romans 1:16, "For I am not ashamed of the gospel, because it is the power of God that brings salvation to everyone who believes: first to the Jew, then to the Gentile."

Ephesians 2:8-9, "For it is by grace you have been saved, through faith—and this is not from yourselves, it is the gift of God—not by works, so that no one can boast."

1 John 5:13, "I write these things to you who believe in the name of the Son of God so that you may know that you have eternal life.

Matthew 28:18-20, "Then Jesus came to them and said, 'All authority in heaven and on earth has been given to me. Therefore go and make disciples of all nations, baptizing them in the name of the Father and of the Son and of the Holy Spirit, and teaching them to obey everything I have commanded you. And surely I am with you always, to the very end of the age."

- What might people say to you after you have shared the Gospel with them? Some will say they are already a Christian (that's good, if true). Some might say they're really not interested (that's good too, because it's honest). Some will look at you and say that you are full of blue mud and it's all non-sense (even that's okay because, remember, Jesus said that would happen). But some, my dear friends, will respond by asking you what they need to do to receive this Jesus that you just described to them.

A simple plan of salvation is all you need in the beginning:
A-B-C's of Salvation

A	**Admit** you are a sinner; repent of those sins
B	**Believe** Jesus died on a cross and 3 days later rose from the dead
C	**Confess** your faith in JESUS CHRIST as your Lord and as your Savior
D (Optional)	At the moment a person places their faith and trust in Christ, they are **Delivered** from the grasp of Satan. They receive another gift, called the Holy Spirit.

Always try and pray with each person that you come in contact with. Prayer shows your compassion. Sometimes once that person sees that you actually care enough about them to hold them up in prayer, they will open up their heart (and ears) to the message you want to share with them.

How to start?

Make a list of people with whom you want to share JESUS.

Look for opportunities about your day to share JESUS.

Be intentional about sharing, make a commitment to God, and then follow through. The Bible says, "When you make a vow to God, do not delay to fulfill it. He has no pleasure in fools; fulfill your vow" (Ecclesiastes 5:4, NIV). If you are going to be intentional about sharing your faith, then do it!! If you are serious, God will constantly keep putting people in your path. But don't say you're going to and then keep putting it off. The Bible says let your yes be yes and your no be no (Matthew 5:37). Make sharing Christ a priority in your life. Watch the blessings begin to flow for you once you are obedient in this area of your Christian walk.

Get your story together, in writing, and then practice, practice, and practice your story until it flows out of your mouth like normal conversation.

After sharing with a lost person, have a plan on how you intend to invite the other person to exercise faith there and then.

And finally, Pray......Pray......Pray.

I have taught this method of sharing the Gospel with countless churches. Over the years, just to be honest, I have sometimes struggled with a bit of the training. Here is why. This life is really not about *us* in any form or fashion. Using the three-minute story method, we are using approximately **two minutes and 15 seconds** to tell somebody about *ourselves* and then using the remaining measly **45 seconds** to tell them about *Jesus Christ*. I believe it's safe to say we have that backwards. This Gospel that we preach and teach must be <u>more</u> about Him and <u>less</u> about us. So why not take two minutes and 15 seconds and tell them the Gospel (Good News) of Jesus Christ and give them an opportunity to be saved just like you and I?

Most of us could easily learn to share the Gospel in less than three minutes. After sharing the Gospel, then take a few seconds to tell them *how* and *why* you got saved. You are basically just affirming to them what you just explained. In other words, it isn't just something that you like to talk about. Rather, you once were lost too and had to hear and respond to the Gospel just like you are asking them to do. This we know for sure; you and I cannot save a soul, but we know the One who can. So, let's do our very best to share the Gospel in an effective and exciting way so that the lost person you are sharing with *wants*, and sees their *need* for, what you are giving to them. Learn to be excited about sharing the greatest news on earth. You believe that, don't you? It absolutely is, hands-down, the greatest story ever. We tell a lot of stories to people that are entertaining, but not life-saving. Why not tell the story, over and over, about the One who sacrificed His own life as payment for our sins, and who rose from the dead, and is alive today?

Here is about a 2 ½ minute Gospel explanation that anybody could learn to share with people. I try to start with a little informal conversation. Hardly anybody enjoys a Christian coming right at them like a freight train. But there is a way to transition from the initial conversation to what you are eventually planning to share with the person. I get to witness quite a bit in large rodeo settings. If I am talking to someone in the vendor area, for example, I might say something like, *"Do you know that if you walked around here long enough, you could find just about anything that you wanted to buy? But I have noticed that there is something that you cannot buy or sign up for here. The answer is your salvation. Your salvation was and is not free."*

After breaking the ice, I might lay the biblical foundation for our need to be saved. For example, *"Seven hundred years before Jesus was born, His birth was foretold. The Bible says in John 3:16 that God so loved the world, that He gave His one and only son, that whosoever believes in Him should not perish but have everlasting life. Jesus is the only way to your salvation. In John 14:6 Jesus says this: I am the way, the truth and the life; no one comes to the Father except through me. My friend, if you want to go to heaven, then we must go through Jesus. Knowledge alone is not enough, but only through a relationship with Him. Jesus Christ was chosen to take your sins on the Cross. In 1 Peter 2:24 it says that He himself bore our sins in his body on the cross, so that we might die to sins and live for righteousness; by His wounds you have been healed. Christ actually means the anointed one or chosen one. Sin is what separates you and me from a Holy God. Romans 3:23 says that all have sinned and fallen short of the glory of God. My friend if you are a living breathing soul, then you are a sinner. But the good news is that God made a way for you to be found righteous in His eyes. Romans 6:23 says that the wages of sin is death, but the gift of God is eternal life in Christ Jesus. So, God gave you a free gift. The gift was His son on the Cross. Jesus died so that you could have everlasting life. The gift of salvation did not cost you a penny, but it cost God His one and only son. The Bible says in Romans 10:9 that if we confess with our mouth that Jesus Christ is Lord and believe in our hearts that God raised him from the dead, that we would be saved."* Now, that is obviously a mouthful, but notice that I said a whole lot in a short amount of time.

After that, you might give 30 seconds of your personal testimony and then leave them with a question. In fact, *always* leave them with a question. For instance, *"When you stand before God to be judged someday, where will you spend your eternity? Is there, in fact, a time and a place when you have asked for Christ's forgiveness and experienced His grace and mercy?"*

For most church people, these are the basics of a Gospel presentation. The Gospel is always the same, but the verses that you may choose to use from time to time will change. My favorite Bible verse is John 14:6, "...I am the way, and the truth and the life. No one comes to the Father except through me" (NIV). I nearly always find a place to share that verse, but there are times I will use other verses as well.

As an evangelist, I have learned to try and read people's body language and to some extent, what they might be thinking as they are hearing the Gospel. It usually isn't that hard to know when someone is interested in the Gospel or not. Their body, their eyes, and their mannerisms will tell you very early on. But I urge you to not give up on telling them the Gospel anyway. If they are allowing you three minutes of their time, take it! Don't put *their* eternal destination on whether *you* can share the Gospel with them "well enough."

We have to leave some room for the Holy Spirit to do His job as well. Remember you and I are never the ones who do the saving (hmm, seems like I have mentioned that several times already). We are here to be faithful and obedient to Christ. If we will focus on our job, then I promise that God will do His job. Amen?

In the outline that I mentioned earlier, you saw the words practice, practice, and practice. This is true. What is your trade right now? Are there any ropers reading this book? Did you start off by catching everything you threw your rope at? No sir. How did you get better at it? Many of us sat out in the back yard throwing our loop on a bucket or a steer head. Then, in time, you moved to your horse and then as even more time went on, you learned to be a fair roper. No matter what you do, practice, practice, practice.

Let us suppose that you are a welder. Think back to when you laid your very first bead. Embarrassing right? So how did your beads get better? You practiced over and over until it finally came to you. No longer are you laying beads, but now you are laying c's. (Only welders will understand this, lol). This is the exact same concept when learning to share the Gospel. You may make all sorts of mistakes and get tongue tied when you first begin, but that is no reason to stop.

The only way you are going to get better is to

continue each and every day. Learn from your mistakes. If you make a conscious effort to share Christ, God will honor that. If you need boldness or courage, ask for it. Look at what Paul says in Philippians 4:6, "Be careful for nothing; but in every thing by prayer and supplication with thanksgiving let your requests be made known unto God" (KJV). God already knows what you need, but He says to make your requests known to Him anyway. Don't be afraid to ask Him to make you bolder, or more courageous, or more in tune with Him so that you can hear what He is trying to say to (and through) you.

Sometimes we make the Gospel so dry that you would have to wonder why anybody would want to accept what you and I are giving to them. If you don't truly believe in what you are saying to somebody, then don't you think they will see right through that? Surely they will. When I am sharing the Gospel, I am always so excited for the opportunity. I mean, after all, there is a chance that if that person is not already saved, that when I am done, they will understand why they need a savior. It's pretty amazing that God allows us to play such a role.

Depending on the person, I may try to add a little humor to the conversation as well. When I have somebody, who seems to be having a pretty good time listening to me and they say "yeah I am pretty sure I am going to go to heaven." I share with them this folly: "Hey are you a good speller? Ok what does S I L K spell? Silk, great. What do cows drink?" Without fail, 98% percent will say "milk." Now that sounds correct, but we know that is not the right answer. Cows drink water. Lol. We set their brain up to say what was already on their mind. When we get done joking about it, I simply say this: "Now you and I can fool each other, but I promise you that neither one of us can fool God Almighty." At that point in the conversation, they truly realize whether they are saved or not. Nobody in their right mind wants to *pretend* that they are saved. Once this is clearly understood, if they know that they are not saved, they are usually ready to do business with God. If God, who is all-knowing and all-powerful knows everything about me, then you and I need to make sure that we are truly saved and truly following the Word of God.

You and I, as servants of the Most High, long to hear these seven words: well done my good and faithful servant. The alternative seven words to hear would be an absolute nightmare: depart from me I never knew you. Your purpose is not to frighten or scare the folks that we are witnessing to, but we do have to be truthful with them and share not only the good, but also the bad. If there is a heaven, then there must be a hell. Whether you believe it or not, it is truth. And it might even be the reality check that certain lost folks desperately need.

My beautiful wife who has been by my side every step of the way.

CHAPTER **5**

God's Monies

HERE IS A little more about Rebecca's and my personal journey as we have sought to follow God's will for our lives. Not everyone has to (nor should!) do this, but we felt strongly led to quit our jobs, step out on faith, and serve the Lord "full-time." A common question we have repeatedly gotten from family and friends is, "How do you support yourselves?" Well that is a great question. There is a Bible verse that we have lived under for a long time. God tells us to walk by faith and not by sight (2 Corinthians 5:7, KJV). When I left the world of cowboying, I also left a steady paycheck at the end of each month. When Rebecca and I decided to answer the call, how would we survive was one of our questions too! How are we going to pay our bills? If God calls you into the ministry, it most likely isn't for you to get rich. It is a call for you to check your faithfulness and your obedience.

When we moved back to Wyoming, I learned that when you start to plant churches, it is important to let the people in your life know what God has called you to do. There are actually churches and individuals who will support the idea of you being a minister of the Gospel. These are things that we had to learn.

I had mentioned along the way that I did not want to be bi-vocational. I wanted to be "all in" and not part-time. Today I understand both ways. It took many years before the financial resources began to come in reliably. This is not to say that we are rich or that we no longer need any support (I am definitely not saying that! Lol.). Rather, this is to say that for the last 10 years, we have lived primarily off of what God has allowed us to receive as love offerings from speaking engagements, monthly support, and one-time gifts.

God is faithful, but I can tell you that this is not an easy lifestyle. We raised three boys while living this way. Yes, we would occasionally pick up some work here and there, but what I found was that the work usually would get in the way of the ministry. Now, when I answered the call of God, I told Him that if I was going to do what He was calling me to do, then I wanted to do it full-time. I was either going to be all in or not in at all. Thankfully, God has answered my plea over and over. As I mentioned, it is not easy, but you definitely *do* learn to rely on God for everything. The acronym for DOG is "depending on God." We have depended every day on God's goodness and faithfulness. We learned that the more faithful we are to God; He is even more faithful to us.

Another comfort we have found in the area of finances is in the Scripture itself. Paul preached to the church of Corinth, and provides great insight as to how ministers of the Gospel should be treated. Check out what he said:

My defense to those who examine me is this: Do we have no right to eat and drink? Do we have no right to take along a believing wife, as do also the other apostles, the brothers of the Lord, and Cephas? Or is it only Barnabas and I who have no right to refrain from working? Who ever goes to war at his own expense? Who plants a vineyard and does not eat of its fruit? Or who tends a flock and does not drink of the milk of the flock? Do I say these things as a mere man? Or does not the law say the same also? For it is written in the law of Moses, 'You shall not muzzle an ox while it treads out the grain. Is it oxen God is concerned about? Or does He say it altogether for our sakes? For our sakes, no doubt, this is written, that he who plows should plow in hope, and he who threshes in hope should be partaker of his hope. If we have sown spiritual things for you, is it a great thing if we reap your material things? If others are partakers of this right over you, are we not even more? Nevertheless we have not used this right, but endure all things lest we hinder the gospel of Christ. Do you not know that those who minister the holy things eat of the things of the temple, and those who serve at the altar partake of the offerings of the altar? Even so the Lord has commanded that those who preach the gospel should live from the gospel. But I have used none of these things, nor have I written these things that it should be done so to me; for it would be better for me to die than that anyone should make my boasting void. For if I preach the gospel, I have nothing to boast of, for necessity is laid upon me; yes, woe is me if I do not preach the gospel! For if I do this willingly, I have a reward; but if against my will, I have been entrusted with a stewardship. What is my reward then? That when I preach the gospel, I may present the gospel of Christ without charge, that I may not abuse my authority in the gospel. (1 Corinthians 9:3-18 NKJV)

Of all the times that I have preached somewhere, at no time (and I mean never) have we required somebody to pay us for our efforts. To be honest, that has sometimes resulted in receiving a handshake and a pat on the back rather than a monetary gift. But for the most part, a majority of God's people know and understand that this is how we have made our living – preaching the Gospel. Even today, there is no other way we would want it. We show up and preach our hearts out, then whatever the congregation or the church feels led to do, that is what we received for the day.

Ministers of the Gospel are no different than most people. They still have bills, are often still raising kids, still have hopes and dreams, and still want a new boat (Okay, that could just be me. Lol.). The point is that the Lord is the giver of all. He *always* meets our *needs*, and more times than I can count, He even meets our wants. That is how crazy the love of the Father can be sometimes. Rebecca and I are always humbled by what God places in our laps. His people (including you, the reader) continue to help support us in a way that allows us to present the Gospel here, there, and everywhere. Thank you! That is our calling. We don't worry about *how* anymore; we just keep moving forward knowing that God is going to supply what we need.

Now, I have made that all sound very simple. And yes, it should be. But there is a human factor in all of this. I suppose the finances is what might have concerned Rebecca more than anything in the beginning. Most women that I know seem to appreciate a stable income. Yes, Rebecca believed, just like me, that God would take care of us, but it is sometimes more easily said than done.

Several years ago, we were truly at the brink of giving up. Our monies were down and we were within one month of being broke. Now I had been very faithful to God in doing my best about being full-time in the ministry. But I had reached my limits. I sat at my desk one day and cried out to God and said, "Lord I cannot live like this anymore. I am 30 days out from having no more money in our ministry account. If things do not change, then I am going to have to take a job and start providing income for my family." I do not recommend a conversation like this with the Lord Almighty. Looking back, I felt like the foolish son looking at the wise dad and telling him just how it was going to be. I would almost call it a temper tantrum. But God being God, heard my prayer that day. He put a couple of people in our path who helped us out financially. I learned that day that my faith had been tested and, unfortunately, I began looking for a way out! Since that day, I no longer test God with our finances. Again, I am not saying that we are wallowing in money (because we're not). But I just don't worry about it like I did. Rebecca and I tend to be very careful with the funds that are entrusted to us for God's work.

We praise God every day that He has connected us with people who are equally passionate about ministering to others and making sure the Gospel is taken to the ends of the earth. Everyone called by God to preach the Gospel needs supporters like that. I wish that ministry could just run on love, but that is simply not the case. Every missionary out there knows exactly what I am talking about. Your support (anyone reading this book) will help the ones who are spreading the Gospel to be able to continue to spread the Gospel. God's people helping out God's people is a win for everyone. Speaking of evangelism...

Rebecca Scott sharing Jesus Christ with 2 contestants at the National High School Finals Rodeo.

CHAPTER 6

Conquering the Fear of Evangelism

THE CALL OF evangelism is not only to evangelists or pastors but to all Christians. The Great Commission tells us so. Matthew 28:18-20 says, "And Jesus came and spoke to them, saying, 'All authority has been given to Me in heaven and on earth. Go therefore and make disciples of all the nations, baptizing them in the name of the Father and of the Son and of the Holy Spirit, teaching them to observe all things that I have commanded you; and lo, I am with you always, even to the end of the age. Amen" (NKJV). It is not an issue of whether or not you *want* to evangelize, or even if you believe you are good at it, or not. Rather, you are commissioned by Jesus Christ to do it.

I always find it motivational to consider some basic math about evangelism. Imagine if one Christian would lead one lost person to the Lord each day for one year. Now imagine if out of those 365 people who got saved, the initial Christian discipled two of them. What if the next year that same Christian again led 365 people to the Lord and discipled two more? As this plays out over a 20-year period, the evangelist eventually will *directly* lead 7,300 people to Christ. That math is rather straightforward and it would be pretty amazing if the story ended there, right? But if the 40 people who were actually discipled did the exact same thing (lead one person per day to Christ and disciple two for 20 years), now from the efforts of that initial evangelist 299,300 people are led to Christ (292,000 from the 40 disciples + 7,300 from the original Christian). That's the size of a fairly large city in America! There are plenty of different directions we could now go with this conversation. What if we discipled more than just two new converts per year? What if we introduced a three-person mentor group?

The numbers above are astounding. Evangelism should lead to multiplication rather than simply addition. If we all get on board, it would result in millions of people being saved. This is not a pipe dream. This is not wishful thinking. This is not a 35-inch Walleye. This is something that God has called us to be a part of. It would be astronomical and miraculous on the one hand, but completely achievable on the other hand. Who is stopping any of us from leading someone to Christ every day? Why couldn't we all take the time to disciple, *really disciple*, two people per year? I believe that God is serious about evangelism and stands ready to supply His power to anyone who is serious about it too.

So, the math is simple. God's Word is clear. On paper, seeing millions come to Christ shouldn't be a problem. Why then do we not see this happening? Especially, we don't seem to see it happening here in the United States. You are probably thinking to yourself, why would he say that? Dear reader, how many people have you led to the Lord this year? We can't complain about how lost society was last year, but then not tell a single soul about Jesus this year. In all of my travels, mission work and preaching, I have only met a small handful of people who actually (and sacrificially) go out of their way to share Christ with others. Now that should make us all upset. Don't be upset with the author of this book; I hear he's a really nice guy, lol. But we need to be upset by what has become normal church and Christian life in America when it comes to evangelism.

Not to keep picking at this scab, but think back for a moment. When was the last time you shared the

Gospel with anyone? In my mind, I cannot make myself understand why most Christians never share Christ. He is the Savior of your soul and for whatever reason, we cannot seem to tell even our closest friends who Jesus Christ is. Now there is something very wrong with that picture. The God of the universe plucked you out of your sin and set you on a narrow road that leads to everlasting life. He gave you a life-changing gift that you didn't deserve, and you can't find the words to tell somebody about Him? How have we managed to let the devil take control of our boldness and courage? The Bible clearly teaches us that God does not put that fear and panic in us.

In 2 Timothy 1:7 the Bible says, "For God has not given us a spirit of fear, but of power and of love and of a sound mind" (NKJV). If you are afraid, it's the devil's doing, not God's. Instead, the Lord gives us the power and the love of a sound mind. So, use it. You can step up to the plate and say: "Devil no more. I am taking back what you have tried to steal from me. I will no longer live a timid life. I will be brave and I will be courageous and I will be strong for the Lord Jesus Christ." Do it. Do it now. Say it out loud. Deal with this before you even bother to read any further. I am pleading with you to take back what the devil has stolen from you for all these years. I know this is the case, because

I have watched many baby Christians share their faith. These are people who in less than one year go under a booth or somewhere downtown and tell others how they came to know Christ and share the Gospel with complete strangers. They are excited about what they are doing. They are excited to share the only way to heaven. I have watched a great many of them, in their first year of being a Christian, lead somebody else to Jesus. Without attending one single theology class or reading any *how-to* books, they just simply begin doing the work of an evangelist and help fulfill the Great Commission. Friends, if a brand-new Christian can do it, you who have been saved for decades can surely do it too.

The number one reason I get from people who say they don't feel comfortable sharing their faith is, "What if they ask me something that I can't answer?" So, what if they do? That's a great thing! It means you're having an actual conversation with a lost person. I get asked questions all the time that I can't give an answer to on the spot. In fact, it's often better not to give a rushed or forced answer on the spot. Ever had one of your kids come to you and say, "Hey, I have a question about my chemistry homework." Most of us would be like, "Uh oh. I have no earthly idea how to help with that." But most of us also know that it isn't good parenting to tell your kids to take a hike and figure it out on their own. It is even worse parenting to not ever engage your children in conversation (spiritual or otherwise) out of fear that they might ask you a question about chemistry. So, what do you do? In my house, the kid would go to bed, and I would jump on the computer and start researching. They would wake up in the morning and I would be feeling like a rock star because I now have the answers they were looking for. Just because you cannot answer a question right off the top of your head, should never be used as an excuse for not wanting to share Christ. I would never brag about this, but the truth is that I probably know at least a tiny bit more about the Bible than the average Christian. But even I sometimes have to say, "Hey, that's a great question. In fact, it is so good that I'm going to have to take a little time to research the correct answer. Most people tend to respect that sort of humility and honesty. Also, people have phone numbers, emails, and addresses. Follow up is not just an option. I highly recommend it!

The truth is, in all of the years of sharing my faith, especially with strangers, people don't typically ask *that* many questions that most born again believers can't answer. Basically, the devil tricks Christians into being fearful about something that usually doesn't even occur. But, to boost your confidence even more, even the best theologians do not know every answer all of the time. They too must sometimes slip back into their quiet place and do a little research and prayer. But this is the way it should be and it is good for everyone involved.

I have found that when I do not know the answer to something, it causes me to have to dig a little deeper. But guess what happens when you start to dig? You find things. You learn more. In fact, you will often learn things that you didn't even know that you needed to know. As somebody who never really enjoyed reading very much or even learning much for that matter (you can ask some of my old school teachers), I have found myself getting enthralled with learning new things, especially from the Bible. The more we learn, the more we grow and the more competent we become. The more competent we become, the more confidence we will have. And all of that will make us much more apt to share Christ more often and in more situations.

A PAUL, a BARNABAS and a TIMOTHY

Let's talk for a moment about who may have been the most inspirational missionary ever to have lived, the apostle Paul. As most of us know, Paul did not start out the way that God wanted him to be. In fact, Paul was previously known as Saul. And Saul was <u>not</u> one of the good guys. Check out what the Scripture says: Acts 7:54-60 says:

> When they heard these things they were cut to the heart, and they gnashed at him with *their* teeth. But he, being full of the Holy Spirit, gazed into heaven and saw the glory of God, and Jesus standing at the right hand of God, and said, "Look! I see the heavens opened and the Son of Man standing at the right hand of God!"
>
> Then they cried out with a loud voice, stopped their ears, and ran at him with one accord; and they cast *him* out of the city and stoned *him*. **And the witnesses laid down their clothes at the feet of a young man named Saul.** And they stoned Stephen as he was calling on *God* and saying, "Lord Jesus, receive my spirit." Then he knelt down and cried out with a loud voice, "Lord, do not charge them with this sin." And when he had said this, he fell asleep. (Acts 7:54-60 NKJV)

That story then carries into the next chapter:

> Now **Saul was consenting to his death**. At that time a great persecution arose against the

church which was at Jerusalem; and they were all scattered throughout the regions of Judea and Samaria, except the apostles. And devout men carried Stephen to his burial, and made great lamentation over him. **As for Saul, he made havoc of the church, entering every house, and dragging off men and women, committing them to prison**. (Acts 8:1-3 NKJV)

Paul did not start out a very good guy. In fact, prior to his conversion to Christ, he was an entirely other person with a completely different name. He viciously persecuted those early Christians, and get this, he did so believing that he was serving God.

Saul was a brilliant man. He was a Pharisee (Acts 22:2-5; Philippians 3:5) who had received his teachings under another Pharisee named Gamaliel, a teacher of the law who was held in respect by all the people. He was not uneducated and he certainly wasn't stupid. But his understanding of God was flawed. God chose to use Saul, but needed to change him first. So, He brought about one of the most remarkable conversions ever to be recorded. The Book of Acts showcases what happens to Saul:

Then Saul, still breathing threats and murder against the disciples of the Lord, went to the high priest and asked letters from him to the syna- gogues of Damascus, so that if he found any who were of the Way, whether men or women, he might bring them bound to Jerusalem. As he jour- neyed he came near Damascus, and suddenly a light shone around him from heaven. Then he fell to the ground, and heard a voice saying to him, "Saul, Saul, why are you persecuting Me?" And he said, "Who are You, Lord?" Then the Lord said, "I am Jesus, whom you are persecuting. It is hard for you to kick against the goads." So he, trembling and astonished, said, "Lord, what do you want me to do?" Then the Lord said to him, "Arise and go into the city, and you will be told what you must do." And the men who journeyed with him stood speechless, hearing a voice but seeing no one. Then Saul arose from the ground, and when his eyes were opened he saw no one. But they led him by the hand and brought him into Damascus. And he was three days without sight, and neither ate nor drank. (Acts 9:1-9 NKJV)

Wow! Do you not think that God got his atten- tion with that? So now Saul must go see a man named Ananias to not only get baptized but to receive back his sight. You can read the remainder of Chapter 9 to get the rest of the details. It is fascinating to me, and I think it is one of the main points of the account, to what depths God is willing to go to "capture" his chosen vessels and to change our hearts in whatever way is needed. But God is God and God can do whatever He deems necessary to get my attention and your attention. Think back to a major event in your life. You might not have been blinded for three days by a bright light (If you were, I would love to hear about it), but has God been seeking to get your attention about becoming more involved in His spiritual plans for humanity? Did you say, as Paul did, "Lord, what do you want me to do" (Acts 9:6, NKJV)?

Saul becomes Paul in the 13th chapter: "Then Saul, who also is called Paul..." (Acts 13:9 NKVJ). From this point on, Saul is always now referred to as Paul. But praise God He did a marvelous work in Paul. Arguably, Paul was the best missionary that ever was. The reason that I want to bring Paul into this picture is to showcase three different kinds of peoples when it comes to evangelizing. You see Paul was never just a one-man band. He had accomplices. He had Barnabas. He had Titus and Timothy. You may have heard this saying before, but in all Christian circles, there should ideally be a Paul, a Barnabas and a Timothy. Let me try and explain.

Paul had the thoughts. He had the knowledge. He knew the things that he was supposed to be doing. But how fun is it to do those things on your own? In my experience, not very! You need, and should want, somebody to experience these things with you. In fact, we are just rarely as effective in ministry when we try to go it alone. We need assistance during the low points, and we need to share the highs with those who helped us get there. Who has God brought to your mind as a partner in ministry? Husbands and wives are a no-brainer. They usually make a great team. However, that isn't what we typically see in the Bible. If you are a woman, who is another woman that you can partner with for the sake of the ministry? God has someone in mind already. Are you praying and attempting to be in-tune with who God would pair you with to be an effective ministry team? If you are man, are you praying that God will reveal another man that you can do ministry with as a team?

Paul was definitely an extrovert. What I am about to share might be a little challenging for an introvert. An introvert is somebody who is often a little closed off to others, which is why surrounding yourself with other ministry partners who have different personalities and different spiritual gifts is usually a good idea. For example, Paul and Barnabas made for a great team. In fact, Barnabas was the first to speak up for Paul. We must remember that others were afraid of Paul after he experienced his conversion, because they still knew him to be the one murdering and putting into prison the apostles and disciples. We see in Scripture:

> And when Saul had come to Jerusalem, he tried to join the disciples; but they were all afraid of him, and did not believe that he was a disciple. But Barnabas took him and brought him to the apostles. And he declared to them how he had seen the Lord on the road, and that He had spoken to him, and how he had preached boldly at Damascus in the name of Jesus. (Acts 9:26-27 NKJV)

So here is where they start to accept Paul as one of the disciples. We all need that one friend who sticks up for us and says, "hey that guy is no longer who he once was."

Praise God, you and I are no longer who we once were. If not, I promise you I would not be writing this book. A passage in 2 Corinthians comes to my mind: "Therefore, if anyone is in Christ, the new creation has come: The old has gone, the new is here" (2 Corinthians 5:17 NIV)!

Man, I am ever so thankful that God picked me up where he had to find me and placed me on a road that is leading straight to Him! Somebody tell me just how good our God is. Amen?!

Ok back to Paul and Barnabas. It says in the book of Acts:

> Then Barnabas departed for Tarsus to seek Saul. And when he had found him, he brought him to Antioch. So it was that for a whole year they assembled with the church and taught a great many people. And the disciples were first called Christians in Antioch. (Acts 11:25-26 NKJV)

Barnabas came along side Paul and helped him teach and disciple these new churches. I don't care what kind of man or woman you are; we need somebody in this life to be on our side to help us with the tasks that the Lord has laid on our hearts.

Surely Christ did not *need* any helpers in his ministry, yet he chose 12 men to play an extremely close part in his life. Something tells me that Jesus was setting an example for us to follow. So, you might not have 12 people, but we should all have one or two. We cannot and really should not be doing this life (let alone kingdom-building ministry and evangelism) on our own. We need somebody to help us build up and encourage others in the faith. But also, and maybe even more importantly, we need somebody to help us when we go through the low times.

One might think that being in the ministry, and serving a glorious God, that every day would be amazing and high. Well that is simply not the case. I will never forget the time that I was sharing the Gospel with one of my old friends. I had been saved a few years and was trying to do what the Bible told me to do. I explained the Gospel to her and asked her if she had ever been saved? Her reply was dumbfounding. She said "saved from what?" I said "your sins." She went on to tell me that she didn't need any kind of saving from anybody. I left that conversation and was deeply saddened. I realized right then that not everybody was going to accept the biblical message of salvation that I had come to believe and had embraced by faith.

I can promise you over the last 10 years of sharing my faith very diligently that I can affirm the frequency of the above type of encounter. There are people out there who don't believe in God, don't see their need for God, don't care about God and, truthfully, will try to make you feel inferior for your belief in God. But don't be discouraged. This is why God has called us to be His witnesses (not because everyone believes, but because so many do not). My encouragement to you is to keep on keeping on, no matter how many times people reject your message. The existence of God and the truth of His message does not depend on how many people believe you when you tell them. God is real no matter what, and your faith is well placed regardless of how many people make fun of you for having it.

When you have had a day that is mind-blowing to you or seems to set you back, you need a Barnabas in your life to help pick you up. Your Barnabas will come along side you and keep your spirits high. The thing about an honest and real Barnabas in your life, is he or she will know when you are feeling low even without you telling them. They learn to read your demeanor. I know in my case that I sometimes don't tell my wife that I have had a rough day. I don't need to, because she can simply feel it and sense it.

Let me give somebody a real nice marriage tip on this. As a man, one of the things that most men want more in their life is the right kind of touch. Most men long for their wives to come up from behind them and for her to wrap her arms around us with her head pressed into our shoulders. For whatever reason, this one motion, just brings comfort to us husbands. Hugging from the front often signals intimacy or romance. But hugging from the back sends a powerful signal of support, encouragement and love (all without saying a word).

What else are the Barnabas's in your life good for? Have you ever had an idea and just thought for a moment, "will this really work?" Is this really worth it? I believe a good Barnabas in your life will help you answer these questions. They are somebody you can bounce ideas off of. In fact, I am certainly no expert in the biblical languages, but I am told that the name Barnabas literally means "son of consolation or son of exhortation." In our English language today, we would say "encourager." That name in itself should give us some idea of what a Barnabas can do. They will encourage you. They will help you. They will "be there" for you.

So, you see, it doesn't matter who you are or what you are doing, every single one of us needs a Barnabas in our lives. So right now, who is your Barnabas? Think carefully. Who helps you with your dreams and adventures in this life? Who is basically like your right-hand man? Who has your back? In military terms, who has your six? Once you figure out who this may be, why don't you tell him or her and show them just how important they are in your life. This is a person that you need to hold onto at almost any cost. Yes, they are *that* valuable and important. After Christ, your Barnabas will serve as a vital anchor for your life.

Turn the conversation around for just a moment.

How would it make you feel for somebody to say to you, "hey I want you to know that you are my Barnabas, or you are my Paul?" Well I can tell you how it feels; it feels pretty darn good. It makes you believe that you are doing what God has called you to do. Then it makes you want to do even more for that person. So, having a Barnabas in your life, will drive you to become a better spiritual servant-leader and be an important part of the puzzle that God is piecing together to further His plans.

Timothy

Now let's move into what a Timothy in your life might look like. Who was Timothy? Timothy was a young man who most likely heard the Gospel when Paul was preaching in Lystra (Acts 16:2-5). Paul saw something in him and spent much time discipling and teaching the young Timothy. There are two books of the Bible directed toward him. There is plenty of valuable information to be gleaned from these two books, but we won't be going into a lot of detail here.

I want to focus in this section on who is your Timothy? I have said this many times before in life: If all we are supposed to do is get saved, then why don't we just get saved and die? Or, even better, why doesn't God just carry us to heaven without dying once we get saved? That makes the most sense to me—a nice short life here then move on to the good stuff for eternity. But most generally, this is not the case. Most people do not get saved and then immediately go to heaven. Yes, there are some deathbed conversions which do result in that scenario. But my guess is if you are reading this book, it means you are probably a Christian (although I certainly hope that non-Christians will read this book too) and that you are probably still alive and living here on planet earth with the rest of us. Why hasn't God taken you "home" yet? Because, you are saved for so much more than just having your ticket punched for heaven. You have knowledge. You have wisdom. You have understanding. You have compassion for the lost. And there are countless folks who need all of that from you. And so, God leaves you here to work and serve. Are we making the most out of our time here? That's the real question.

So, like Paul, in order to be as effective as we need to be while serving God in this world, we too need a Timothy (or Timoth<u>ies</u>) in our lives. I think this is especially true for the older generation. They sometimes believe (wrongly, very wrongly, extremely wrongly) that they are simply too old to be any good anymore. I cannot stress enough just how far from the truth that is. The Bible says, "The silver-haired head is a crown of glory, if it is found in the way of righteousness" (Proverbs 16:31 NKJV). If you have silver hair, grey hair, or maybe even at this point you don't have any hair at all, I believe this verse is speaking to you. You have wisdom that younger folks do not yet have. It has not been given to them yet. They have not lived enough life for their knowledge and understanding to evolve into wisdom. So, for you who say that you are too old, that my friend is nothing more than a cop-out. However, you might benefit greatly from adding a Timothy to your life. My friend, when GOD thinks you are too old to be of any use, then maybe He will take you home. But until then, there is work to be done. Get out of the rocking chair, find your Paul, Barnabas, and Timothy, and get busy for God.

Some of you have fallen asleep in your days, and it is high time to awake, arise, and redeem the time. Ephesians 5:14-16 says, "...Wake up, sleeper, rise from the dead, and Christ will shine on you. Be very careful, then, how you live—not as unwise but as wise, **making the most of every opportunity**, because the days are evil" (NIV). The English Standard Version says, "...**making the best use of the time...**" Guess what? When Christ is shining His light upon you, then it is your duty and your obligation to shine that light for others to see as well. Time is of the essence. You are not dead. You are definitely alive if you are reading this book. I don't even have to ask you to check your pulse. But

I am asking you to make some changes in your life. Yes, maybe you are older, but older does not mean dead. You have so much to offer to the youngers of this world. As I am writing this book, there is rioting, looting, and violence going on all across America and the world. People need the Light! People need godly love and wisdom shown to them and modeled for them, and WE are the ones called to do it.

What does it look like today to be a Paul to a Timothy? There is a saying that I once read that said children spell love T I M E. I believe it to be the same for our Timothies. If you and I are truly going to make disciples then we must be willing to give of our time. This will look different for each person reading the book. Time is something that each of us have. In fact, every living person has the same amount of allotted time each day: 24 hours, or 1,440 minutes or 86,400 seconds—however you want to look at it. The only difference is how people spend that time and when God brings your time to a close.

The adage that says however much you put into something will be what you get out of it holds very true for making disciples. Disciple-making takes time. It takes time away from your "fun" activities and it takes time away from your family. So, this time must be managed in a thorough way. There has to be balance, but truthfully, most of us have more spare time than we typically admit. For most of us, we have the early mornings or later in the evenings that we can give to making disciples. The majority do not have the time to leave their jobs in the middle of the afternoons. So, use your time wisely, especially if you are setting up a once-per-week, or even better, twice-per-week meeting with the person that you are discipling. I realize that some people's schedules are not always conducive to a regularly scheduled meeting. All I can say is to do the best that you can. Most Christians, sadly, are not taking the time to disciple anybody, so any amount of time and effort you can make will be better than nothing.

For the men, I have found it to be very rewarding (and productive) to take the person that you are discipling outdoors. Being an avid outdoorsman, I find numerous ways to reach and teach the younger men about Jesus in this type of setting. I love to fish. I have joked before that once I have you in my boat, unless you can walk on water like Jesus, then you are going to have to listen to what I may have to say. But it is never actually like that. When you get somebody alone, their demeanor typically changes. If I have the opportunity to witness to five men in their 20's verses one man in his 20's, I will take the single every time. Because, when most men are in a group, testosterone tends to be part of the dynamic. One often tries to out-do the next and there is just simply more resistance than normal. But once you have them alone the lack of peer pressure seems to help them reason and think differently. They are more apt to be open and honest. If you are honest and level with them, in return, they will usually reciprocate.

So, if you love the outdoors, then share that with the person you are teaching and training. There are many lessons to be learned from being outside. Fishing is typically very relaxing. They are either biting or they aren't. Sitting on a boat all day, gives you many opportunities to say what you want to say to them.

Hunting is a little different. If you are on a stand somewhere, there may not be much talking going on. If you are scouting around in a pickup or just simply hiking in the mountains, you have more time to visit. Taking the life of an animal will always be the source of a great conversation. Life and death—What is the meaning? It is a great time to talk about this life and their death. It won't be any more real to them than when an animal has just given its life for you or him. It is very real and it is vivid.

Maybe you like to ride a bicycle, go jogging, or play tennis or golf. Whatever your hobbies are, take your Timothy with you. Involve them in your activities so that they can have that all-important T I M E with you. It is one thing to lead a Bible Study. That is good, obviously, and important. But it is another thing for baby Christians to see exactly how you, the experienced, wise, obedient and faithful Christian handle other areas of life, including leisure time.

I have seen it several times while ministering in Africa. People who are hungry for the Word of God, want your time above all else. I have taught in Africa until my voice was almost gone. They didn't care. They wanted to continue to learn more and more from the Word. If you tell them that you will teach them two lessons, they will want three and then four. It is not like it is here in the United States. Village people have no concept of time. It is either day or night. If it is day, then they stay busy. When you are teaching, there is no watch-looking. I suspect this is most likely for two reasons: (1) most do not even know what a watch is and (2) they simply don't care about the time. They want to learn as much as you are willing to teach them.

Sometimes that is why it is important to take your teaching and training outside of the church or a building. There is a psychology involved here, at least in the United States. When you "go to church" there is an expectation that the "service" or activity will last only a specific length of time, usually an hour or an hour and fifteen minutes. But when you take someone fishing, as I mentioned before, that could last all day long and the other person wouldn't be surprised and most likely wouldn't even care. Again, this I know for sure for the guys. Many men just learn better or get it more when outside. It could be that many of the ladies enjoy more of a traditional setting—I don't know. Either way you choose to do it, the bottom line is if you want to see somebody being discipled, then you must first be willing to give your <u>time</u> to that person.

One verse that I want you to keep in your minds when teaching and training is found in 2 Timothy 2:2, "And the things that you have heard from me among many witnesses, commit these to faithful men who will be able to teach others also" (NKJV). Commit this verse to your memory and recall it when times get tough. Because, at some point in the discipling process, it will get rough and most likely after that, it will get even rougher still. For example, your Timothy might, out of the blue, say they don't want to be discipled anymore. Sometimes the Timothy's unbelieving family or friends will become an obstacle in the discipling process. Sometimes your own sinful nature will say that you are spending "too much time" away from your own life. And many times, you will just prefer to be doing other things on that particular day. It could be any number of issues, but fall back on this verse from 2 Timothy and let it bring you through the tough times. The end product is what you have to keep in mind. Your faithfulness, at some point, is bound to have an incredible impact on somebody's life as well as your own.

I can share extremely personal and extremely painful examples from my own life and ministry. The reason I am about to write what I am about to write is because, I figure, if I have experienced these feelings then my guess is that others have too. It is hard to count the number of times I have said to myself, "James, there are other things you could be doing." On many occasions, I have failed at making the time that is needed to disciple somebody. Here are some excuses that I wrestle with on a regular basis (yes, still to this day): It is too late and I have already had a long enough day. I have not had enough time to sit down and study what I am supposed to teach tonight. I am already scheduled to go to *these* meetings today and *those* events tonight; I won't have any energy left for discipling. Or, how about this one? They probably won't show up anyway, so I'll just cancel. Is that lame or what? Can you relate to these or even others that are not mentioned here?

All of us are usually pretty good at making up excuses as to why we don't have the time to disciple. However, we have already established how many hours there are in each day. It is true that there are only 24 hours each day, rather than 34 or 44 or 54. But, 24 hours is a lot and it only requires a little bit of planning to squeeze the most out of those 24 hours, IF we really want to. The truth is that we have the time to disciple a new believer, but we often don't for one lame reason or another (and then usually blame it on a lack of time). In our minds, hey, we gave it a try. But not really. We really didn't *try* at all. The famous western actor John Wayne had a saying in the movie, *The Cowboys*, "trying don't get it done son." If we truly try, then don't you think we could actually see some results from *honest* efforts? That should be the case, but the reality of it is that we did not try very hard.

I have said this so many times before. If it was important to us, then we would have made the time for it. Do you agree? Matthew 6:21 says, "For where your treasure is, there will your heart be also (KJV). Most people think this just means money. But we can "treasure" a lot more than just our bank account. But the things that we treasure speak volumes about where our heart is on a particular subject. Where is your treasure? If you wanted to disciple that person today, you would have. But some of us are really good at making excuses. Let me pick on the men here for a minute. Let's suppose your wife calls and asks you to do something helpful when you get home. Your reply is that it has been a long day, but maybe you can get to it tomorrow. Your married son or daughter calls and they need you to fix this or that at their house, and again, you are just simply too tired so you decline. Your children meet you at the door with homework in hand and once again, you are too tired to even help them with a problem. Does any of this fly?

Now watch this. Your buddy calls and needs help pulling an engine. They are the fourth person in line to call on your help that night and you get in the truck and run right over there. Or, your buddy calls you two hours before dark and says, "hey man the crappies are biting, you should get down here." You and your fishing pole are loaded and headed to the lake to meet him. It takes you about two minutes to get loaded and headed out. How about this one? It is deer season or turkey season and your trail camera (that is linked to your cell phone, of course), sends you a message and shows you what is coming into your stand. All of your tiredness is mysteriously gone as you grab your gun and head out the door. But if God "calls you up" and nudges you to go share the Gospel or to disciple a new believer, all of a sudden, we are too tired or too busy again.

I am pretty convinced that I have just stepped on a zillion toes at this point. We could not be bothered for anything that our *families* wanted us to do, but if it was something that *we* wanted, we were no longer tired and we were ready to jump aboard with no questions asked. What you treasure reveals where your heart is (Matthew 6:21). You can read that verse again and again. Let it sink in until it begins to hurt. But it will be the good kind of hurt, because good old-fashion conviction by the Holy Spirit is what spurs us to change our attitudes and behavior. For where your treasure is, there your heart will be also. You see, men (and women), we do what we *want* to do, and we do what *we* think is valuable and important. We do the things that we treasure without delay and we give it our all. Now, we just need to learn to value what God values the most.

Those things that I mentioned above (car engines, fishing, hunting, etc.) are not bad in any way. In fact, they are a lot of fun. But where is your sense of responsibility? Take care of what God has given to you each and every single day. If you are faithful to take care of your family, to take care of your loved ones, to take care of the one or two people that you may be discipling, then I believe God will honor your obedience with time to do all of those other things (within reason, of course). Living life the right way requires finding balance. When we allow our lives to get out of balance, then guess what happens? It is very tough to get it back to where it should be. It's sort of like gaining weight. It is very easy to add the pounds, but incredibly hard to fight back to where you were before you allowed the bad habits to creep in. So, make the time to disciple the people that God has put in your path. Make the time to help your spouse, your children, your buddies, and yes, even schedule a little down time for yourself. Learn what balance looks like in your life. Strive to keep that balance. Why? Because, most everyone reading this book right now knows what life is like when it gets out of balance. Unbalanced will eventually lead to ungodly. I would say that most of us (author included) can testify to what that looks like.

I have been ungodly before, and it's a place I never want to go back to. Think of a time (notice I said a time and not all the times – I don't want to embarrass anybody too much, lol) when you were outside of the will of God AND you were very well aware of it. How did you feel? The Holy Spirit, of course, convicts us when we stray, and if He works on you anything like He works on me, it is almost instantaneous. We know that we know that we are outside of the will of God. For me, personally, it is like a feeling of being unsettled or constantly a feeling like walking on egg shells. I have been both on the inside of God's will and outside of His will. My prayer is that I never have to experience the outside again.

What a feeling it is to be under the wings of your heavenly father (Psalm 61:4). We should want to be there, but this also happens to be where *He* wants *us* (Luke 13:34). It is hard to describe how amazing it is to voluntarily be exactly where God wants us to be. This all circles back around to our larger discussion of Matthew 6:21. You will make the time for the things you want to do or accomplish. You will make the time for the relationships that you want or desire. You will make the time for the things that attract your heart. Why not, then, just adopt the list of things and people that fit into God's will for your life, rather than going in your own direction?

Let's sum up this section. Every believer needs to figure out exactly where your highest priorities and deepest desires are. Why? Because it reveals where your heart is. Our hearts will either follow after the world, or the things of God (Romans 12:2). Notice exactly where God has set your boundaries. Get inside the will of God and stay THERE!!! It truly is the best place for all of us to be. If you are being called by God to disciple someone (hint, you almost certainly are), then make sure that becomes a priority in your life. It is a blessing to be able to watch somebody grow from a baby Christian into a mature and fully functional, re-producing follower of Jesus Christ.

In case you need even more biblical persuasion, consider the following Bible verses: 1 Peter 2:2 says, "As newborn babes, desire the sincere milk of the word, that ye may grow thereby" (KJV). Also, the Apostle Paul told the Corinthians that he gave them milk, not solid food, because they were not yet ready (1 Corinthians 3:2). The mature Christian is at the front of each of these verses. They know what it is like to be overfed and they know what it's like to still be drinking milk. This is the wisdom that we spoke of earlier. It is why it is so important for you, not somebody else, but for you to be a disciple-maker.

Newborn Christians are not that much different from newborn babies. They need to be nurtured. A baby has to drink milk before they can graduate on to tastier, and frankly, healthier food. Who is going to help them transition from milk to solid foods? Here is the problem that I see. We, mature Christians, have done a lousy job of discipling our new believers. How can I be so cruel as to say such a thing, you might ask? Easy. We have men and women who supposedly came to Christ 20 years ago, 30 years ago, or even 40, 50, and 60 years ago who are still running around drinking out of a sippy-cup instead of eating ribeye steaks from the Bible. That's right, God has steak on the menu, but grown adults who were converted, sometimes, decades in the past, <u>prefer</u> drinking milk from a sippy cup rather than taking up a fork and knife. We are not discipling our people and the negative effects of that are devastating our churches across the land.

I'll use myself as another example. Right after my wife and I got saved, the small-town church that we were attending folded up. I mean, it went from seemingly healthy to closed down, all the way, period. Because of that, my wife and I were never discipled. This church had its pastor called up to the military, and that was it. Thinking back, I have often asked myself, "where were the men that could have and should have stepped up to keep our little church afloat?" Maybe they were never discipled either. I may never know the full story, but that is another reason why I take this whole discipling thing very seriously.

Think about your own level of spiritual maturity right now. Who discipled you? How much do you truly know about the Scriptures, the stories, the Bible characters and anything else that is associated with maturing into a fully functional Christ-follower? The church as a whole has failed badly at this.

We sometimes reach people outside of the church, get them to attend, lead them to Christ, and get them baptized. And then, often as quickly as they arrived, they seem to strangely fade away, sometimes, never to be heard from again. Where did they go? Do we even care? Sometimes the church judges those brand-new believers very harshly and even blames them for not being "faithful enough" to stick with the program. But it was not *their* job to be mature and wise enough to do the right things when they were only months, weeks, or even just days into their Christian walk. It was the *church's* job to provide guidance, love, and discipleship. So, again, where do these people go when they leave the church? Sometimes not very far at all. They could easily be found if mature Christians would bother to look for them.

This is not simply a numbers game, but let's get down to business and think about the kind of numbers that would be pleasing to God. If He tells us that we are to make disciples "of all the nations" then surely we are talking about large numbers. Again, it is the last thing Christ told His followers to do before He departed this earth for heaven. We call it the Great Commission. "Then Jesus came to them and said, "All authority in heaven and on earth has been given to me. Therefore go and make disciples of all nations, baptizing them in the name of the Father and of the Son and of the Holy Spirit, and teaching them to obey everything I have commanded you. And surely I am with you always, to the very end of the age" (Matthew 28:18-20 NIV). Do you now see why this is so dog gone important? It is a command.

It is not a push from some evangelist from Wyoming who's trying to tell you to go do something. It is a full-on command from the Lord Jesus Christ not only to His initial disciples but also to us. Go and make disciples.

There are going to be a great number of Christians who read this book who have not yet made a single disciple. My friend, you are missing out. I can somewhat liken it to a good ranch horse, or a fine-tuned bird dog. You put all this training into the critter and someday, all of that training pays off. You are able to watch your hard work get put into action. You play a pivotal part in that. You get to sit back and watch "your" prodigy do what you have trained them to do. It is a great and wonderful feeling.

Do not boast, but be proud in the Lord for the commitment you made to that new Christian and the quality time you invested in them. This is the best way that I can try and describe this training relationship. You put all of this time and effort into somebody and someday you will watch them grow into a fine young man or woman who has become a warrior for Christ. When that happens, you have done your job. Now, maybe you can take up the rocking chair, because you accomplished your mission. Just kidding! Your mission is to find another. Your mission is to make disciples (plural). What do you do when you finish reading the Bible? Do you put

it on the shelf and never look at it again? Heck no!!!!!
Start over from the beginning, or study a particular passage or book. Never stop reading, studying, applying, and obeying. The same is true when discipling. When you are "finished" with one believer (although they may still be asking you questions for <u>years</u> to come), find somebody else. Wash, rinse, and repeat. Discipling is a process that never ends. It must be like a revolving door for your life. It isn't a "task" that you check off, or a goal that you accomplish. It must be a way of life.

I have a great friend named Rhyan Boesen. I met Rhyan when he was only about 14 years old on a ranch out in Wyoming. He was a likeable kid but knew nothing whatsoever about spiritual things. For years we stayed in contact with him and roughly 10 years ago, after many times of sharing the gospel and witnessing to him about Jesus Christ, we heard from him around midnight one night. He called on the phone, we talked, and then my great friend Rhyan asked God to forgive his sins and asked Christ to be his Lord and Savior. That was the night that Rhyan got saved. It was glorious.

Here are some fun details about Rhyan (shared with his permission, of course) and a testament to just how fast the Holy Spirit can do His job. Rhyan was living with his girlfriend/fiancé at the time in Missouri. Two days after his conversion, he called me and said, "James, when can you come and marry my fiancé and me?" We were about 1100 miles apart at the time and my schedule was not going to allow me to just drop everything that I was doing and run to Missouri to marry this couple. He explained to me that after he had gotten saved, there was no way he could continue doing what he was doing with his fiancé and not be married. He felt he was living in a sinful relationship and earnestly wanted to correct that. He called me within two days and said that because they were under conviction, they had gone down to the courthouse and eloped. They made a commitment to God and have been happily married ever since.

Fast forward about 10 years. Rhyan is now an absolute warrior for Jesus Christ. Most everyday he is having Jesus-conversations with somebody somewhere. He gets it. He has realized the importance of being discipled and then going out and sharing his faith.

God blesses our efforts. He finds favor on His children. Right before the publication of this book, Rhyan was leading Bible studies and discipling men so that they too could become soldiers for Christ. That is discipling at its finest and fits perfectly with a verse we already looked at once. "And the things that you have heard from me among many witnesses, commit these to faithful men who will be able to teach others also" (2 Timothy 2:2 NKVJ). That is how it should work – one soul at a time being discipled. Then, after *being* discipled, you my friend become the one *doing* the discipling. But what an absolute blessing it is that God allows us to play such a key role in the discipleship process.

Here is another quick story that came out of Rhyan being saved. Our youngest son, Dylan, was 11 years old at the time. While I had been witnessing to my friend Rhyan , I had no idea that my own son was listening to me from a distance. My wife nearly killed me when I told her I was going to recount this story accurately, with ALL of the truthful details included. Here goes… My wife was on the potty before bed one evening. As she sat there on the throne (yes, I know, I already said she nearly killed me, lol). But as she sat there, a slip of paper came sliding under the door. Our 11-year-old had written on a piece of paper that he did not want to go to hell when he died. He literally wrote a note asking his mother, when she was done, if she could pray with him so that when it was his turn to die, he would go to heaven. As my wife read the note, tears fell from her eyes. She left the bathroom and came and showed me the note. We were both elated. We went to his room, knelt down by his bed, and God allowed us to lead our 11-year-old son to Jesus. It was a powerful and unforgettable moment.

The next morning, I excitedly called my friend Rhyan and shared with him that not only did he receive salvation last night, but our son called on the name of Christ as well! Again, more tears were shed and God was glorified. This story shows us the power of not only witnessing to the person that you are intentionally aiming at, but sometimes we have no idea who is eavesdropping on our conversations. But this was a great eavesdrop. We must remember that sometimes God has others within ear shot, to hear the Good News as well.

I have remembered this concept very well. When we first started preaching, we would be at some very small, county fair style rodeos. There might have only been 30 to 40 people in the stands right in front of me, but I would always set up the loud speakers and wear a lapel mic anyway. Why? It wasn't for the small crowd in front of me. It was for the guy or gal brushing their horse across the arena or the couple who were sitting in their lawn chairs enjoying a cup of coffee at their horse trailer. Just because they are not directly in front of you, doesn't mean that somebody somewhere else is not listening to what is being said. Maybe the *parents* did not want to attend but the *children* wanted to see why there was a small group of folks sitting at the bleachers. For whatever reasons people might have for "eavesdropping," we must be mindful of those ears as well as the ears sitting right in front of us. We never know the effect of our echoing words!

My son Dylan being prepared for a life flight helicopter ride after his devastating horse accident.

CHAPTER 7

Backsliding

LET ME SHARE a story of what backsliding and rededicating your life might look like when put in the perspective of life and death. Our youngest son, Dylan, got saved when he was 11 years of age. As he went through his teenage years, he had two older brothers to look up to. Well, growing up on a ranch and being around cowboys and ranchers all the time, Dylan picked up the bad habit of chewing tobacco. We busted him several times, and one of the last times we caught him we sat him down at the dining room table and had a "come to Jesus" conversation with him. Dylan had a car at the time so we let him decide his fate: He could lose his car for one month or we could take away his phone for a month if he continued to chew tobacco. He chose not to drive for a month.

July 11, 2017 changed our whole family's life. Dylan,

Rebecca, and I went up a mountain to help a neighbor move their cows to higher pastures. We only had two horses at the time, so Dylan rode one of the neighbor's horses. Please note that all three of my kids grew up riding nearly every day. They could ride almost anything. So, Dylan started riding from the corral while Rebecca and I drove up a couple of more miles before we unloaded our horses to start gathering the cows. I would say we had been split up for at least an hour or so. We finally met up with Dylan at the bottom of a big draw. He said (I'll never forget), "Dad, this horse is being a knot head." I said, "Can you handle him?" Dylan just nodded his head and rode off.

Here's when things changed. At this point, we were behind a bunch of cattle with several other cowboys and cowgirls. As I went around to the left side of the cows, I heard the most dreadful scream a father could ever hear, "DAAAAAAAAAAAAAADDDDDDDDDD DDD!!!" As I turned my horse around, I saw Dylan's horse running full speed without Dylan. I ran as fast as I could to get to my son. What I saw when I got there was terrifying. He was curled up in somewhat of a ball and blood was flowing from his mouth. I was in shock but I had to do something. He could not speak. He laid there almost lifeless. I typically don't ride with a cell phone but for some reason I had it in my pocket (cue throat-clearing noise as we all acknowledge that was a God thing). I immediately called 911. Now where we were located, you could not get a vehicle to, so they had to send a helicopter to come for our son. It took paramedics about an hour to reach our location.

While I lay on the ground trying to console our son and tend to his injuries, I had one of the other cowboys go get Rebecca. She was about two ridges over. Dylan could not say a word. We truly had no idea of the extent of his injuries. I had never seen a member of my own family in this much misery. He motioned for his phone because he couldn't talk. I looked on the ground and found his phone. He texted these words to me: "I have not been living my life right, dad, and in case I don't make it, I want to get right with God right now." So, right there, on top of that mountain in the bottom of big ole draw, I prayed aloud while Dylan prayed from his heart and asked God to forgive him and set him back on the right road. I saw Dylan's tears as they streamed down the face of a very scared young man. As we got done praying, he reached for his sock. In his sock was a can of chewing tobacco. He texted me that he knew he was going to lose his car for a month. I tossed the can of chew and said, "you just get through this."

As he lay there motionless, I could see his mom coming towards us on a pretty good lope. As she got closer, all she could see was her son's lifeless body lying there. She started screaming my name in horror. She jumped off her horse and ran to her baby boy. She was crying profusely. I was assuring her that he was okay for the moment, but we didn't know where all the bleeding was coming from. She hovered over and loved on her baby in the way that any mom would do if their baby was hurt. Have you noticed that it doesn't much matter the age of a child for the baby to still be a baby even at 17 years of age?

As the time approached for the life flight helicopter to land, the cowboys moved all our horses several hundred yards away. Dispatch had told me on the phone that when the pilot circled to land, to be sure to shield our son with our bodies because it would be very loud and windy. Boy were they right! We had never been around a helicopter this close before. The helicopter landed and they immediately went to work on our son, preparing him for the trip to Billings, Montana. After they secured him on a stretcher and had his head immobilized, four of us picked up our son and carried him to the nearby chopper. It was a horrendous feeling, knowing what our son was going through and what he was about to have to go through. We got him loaded, and I insisted that we all pray right there. We prayed and watched as they took our son up into the sky. To this day, I will never forget the look on my wife's face as she watched her baby fly away.

We then immediately jumped on our horses and headed to the trailer as fast as we could. Now, you have to imagine for a moment just how steep this draw was. Tall sagebrush and the sheer steepness made it a slow go to get up out of where this all happened. I remember stopping for a moment to let our horses catch their breath. I turned to my wife and said these words: "No matter what happens with our son, you and I must promise each other right here and right now that we will stay together." As a pastor, I have read the statistics on marriages after the death of a child. Nearly 90% end in divorce. I did not want that to even enter our minds. We both agreed then finished the ride back to our truck and trailer.

Some of the other cowboys had already unhitched our trailer and brought our truck as close as they could for us. We jumped off the horses, said thanks and drove like crazy for almost 3.5 hours to get to Billings. And for those incredibly long 3.5 hours, we had zero contact with our son or the hospital. Not having an update of any kind was extremely painful, to say the least. We finally arrived at the hospital and they immediately took us to our son. They started to explain that all the blood was coming only from his mouth. We had feared internal injuries, so we praised God for His mercy! Dylan's face had been shattered. He had five breaks in his face, a broken sacrum, and a big contusion on his head.

When it was all said and done, he had his jaw wired shut for nearly six weeks. He also went through several months of rehab to get his back to heal properly. Praise God he had no *physical* life-altering injuries, but it was a tremendous *spiritual* experience for the whole family.

Toward the end of his healing time, Dylan wrote a poem. Now that in itself blew us away! Where we live, 17-year-old boys do not write poems very often! The first time I ever read it, I was in church. I had just preached a message, and told the whole story of Dylan's horse accident. He sent the poem to me on my phone just minutes before I was to preach, so I wasn't able to read it ahead of time. As I ended the sermon, I explained to the congregation that he had written a poem and that I had never read it and was going to read it for them. This poem is called "The Horse," by Dylan Scott:

There the steed lays as I see in my dreams
Bronze like a golden watch ticking fast
Perks his ears as he hears my screams
Stands up quick with his feet in a solid stance
The look in his eyes are filled with sorrow
He emits a powerful glow of light and heat
He comes forward onto me like tomorrow
I feel the weight of him like I was a seat
I wake up in the hard dirt and the blood

I felt hotness all over my legs and face
The pain and fear hit me like a flood
I wake up in a small noisy flying case
I come out with steel strings and a metal plate
I thank the Lord that that wasn't my final fate

Again, I was in front of an entire church congregation when I read this for the first time. So, naturally, I cried like a baby. My voice cracked so hard I don't even know if they could hear all of the words. We had learned that what caused all of the injuries to our son was the horse reared up and came over backwards on him. The saddle horn, both hurt him and saved him. The doctors later told us that if the horn would have caught him in the heart area, it could have killed him instantly. Instead, the saddle horn was driven into his mouth and crushed his jaw and surrounding area.

Rebecca, Dylan, and I (and I'm sure others as well) will never forget this incident. It is a reminder to all of us that we are not immune from accidents, pain, and loss. Our lives can change in the blink of an eye. We are truly only one phone call from our knees. But no matter what the circumstances are, believers must always find ways to give God honor and glory no matter the circumstances. My son, a year later, told us that what he missed the most, when his jaw was wired shut, was talking (not eating, but talking). That was ironic to Rebecca and me, because of all three of our children, Dylan was the one who spoke the least. The accident changed his life in this very important way. He can now speak to almost anybody, which means that he is even more *usable* for God. There is always something good that comes from every situation. We just have to be keen enough to look and faithful enough to let God open our eyes to it.

Let me also add to this that Rebecca and I made one post about Dylan's horse accident on our Facebook page. From one post we literally had tens of thousands of people praying for our son. There is power in prayer. People literally stopped what they were doing and prayed to God on Dylan's behalf. It mattered. We felt it. We are humbled and grateful.

Paul wrote, "Do not be anxious about anything, but in every situation, by prayer and petition, with thanksgiving, present your requests to God. And the peace of God, which transcends all understanding, will guard your hearts and your minds in Christ Jesus" (Philippians 4:6-7 NIV). How relevant were these verses? People were praying and we were praying, and we had this powerful sense of peace that Paul was talking about.

Paul also told the Galatians that we ought to carry one another's burdens in order to fulfill the law of Christ

(Galatians 6:2). Throughout it all, we felt as if there were people carrying our burden with us. Although it was a very scary time in our lives, it was a glorious time to watch the Lord's people come around us and minister to us. Rebecca and I had been ministering to people for years, and then God saw fit for many of those same people to now minister to us. But complete strangers were also lifting us up to the Lord through it all. For example, I received a phone call from a man. To this day, I still don't even know who it was. He called me and said, "James, you don't know me, but I want to pray with you for your son." That phone call blew our minds. Wow! God's people are awesome. Thank you, Lord!

Okay, that was a very lengthy story just to talk about backsliding. But our son, within minutes of his accident and while still lying in a puddle of blood, knew that he had let his Christian walk slip and he earnestly wanted to correct it. These types of reminders happen. I wish they didn't have to happen in such a painful way, but God simply works that way sometimes. And honestly, it is better to be prompted by God in a painful way, than to not be prompted by God at all.

Some people consider "backsliding" as <u>losing</u> their salvation. I do not hold that position at all. I don't believe you can lose your salvation, and here's why:

Jesus answered them, I told you, and ye believed not: the works that I do in my Father's name, they bear witness of me.

But ye believe not, because ye are not of my sheep, as I said unto you.

My sheep hear my voice, and I know them, and they follow me:

And I give unto them eternal life; and they shall never perish, neither shall any man pluck them out of my hand.

My Father, which gave them me, is greater than all; and no man is able to pluck them out of my Father's hand. (John 10:25-29 KJV)

Ever since I was saved (over 20 years ago now), I have mostly attended Baptist churches. Now, if you are a staunch Baptist, you know the saying that I am about to say: "once saved always saved." That is of course true if you are truly saved. I prefer to say, "once saved always saved if saved." I think that makes much better sense.

Many people are walking around this world thinking they are saved, but the sad reality is that many of them likely are not. Why? Because there is more to being saved than just praying a little prayer, walking an aisle or even just raising your hand when an evangelist tells you to. I have seen this time and time again, especially at youth events. The speaker gives an invitation and your buddy eithers walks down the aisle or looks at you and says something like, "what do you think, should we go or not?" Now if those two both go, *maybe* one of them is sincere about putting their trust and faith in Jesus Christ. But what about the guy who is walking an aisle just because his buddy chose to? Or, they go forward because some pretty girl is doing it and he thinks, "Well, I just as well be in the group that has the pretty girl." Where is the relationship in that? I have seen evangelists say raise your hand if you want to be saved. Some out in the crowd raise their hands and by some magic, the evangelist announces to them that they are now saved. That is about as far from the biblical idea of salvation by faith alone in Christ alone as you can possibly get. That practice needs to end.

It isn't just kids, either. Plenty of adults allow their emotions to get stirred up at church, a revival, or some religious event. But, getting saved is <u>not</u> about an emotion. Getting saved is about you recognizing that you are a sinner and that you need a savior and that the only true Savior's name is Jesus Christ.

Let's say you do get saved and truly have an encounter with Christ. Praise the Lord. But then life happens, and you fall straight back on your face. Are you still saved? Yes, absolutely. Look at Peter in the Bible. Jesus himself once called Peter "Satan" (Mark 8:33). You can mess up and still be saved. Look at David in the Old Testament. It seems like at different times of his life, he broke just about every commandment that God ever gave. Yet, God still called David a man after His own heart (Acts 13:22). Messing up is a part of this life. But in order to backslide you have to be saved first. You can't backslide if you have never been saved. Otherwise, you are simply just still lost. That is a big difference, obviously. Being saved doesn't mean you don't mess up or ever sin again. It would be awesome if that were the case. But that is not the case in <u>this</u> life. Of course, for the Christian, everything is going to be perfect in the <u>next</u> life. I am looking forward to that just as much as anyone else!

We have already made mention of this verse, but Romans 3:23 tells us that, "for all have sinned and fall short of the glory of God" (NIV). Friends, all means all. You have no choice in the matter. You were born with a nature that instinctively resists the things of God. But when it comes to daily life, there is still a difference between willfully disobeying God and making some dumb choices occasionally. We all do stupid things once in a while, but to willfully disobey the Father, that is plain ole sin at its finest.

You could argue that backsliders make stupid choices *and* willfully disobey God from time to time. I would agree with that. But here is what some might be missing. I can say this because I have lived both ways. When you are living <u>inside</u> of the will of God, meaning you are continually with all efforts trying to do what is pleasing to Him, your life will have great blessings. I know this first hand. Of course, why wouldn't God want to bless you for following His lead in life? Then at other times in my life, many years ago, I could have taught a class on the best ways to be <u>outside</u> of the will of God. Believe me, there are no blessings there, nor should we expect there to be.

We obviously know that backsliders are a reality in the world. Some of you still reading might have been a backslider or might be backsliding right now. It's okay (actually it's not okay but it is fixable). I know before I was sold out to Christ, I most likely back slid. But today is different. When a person sells out it means they are 100% sold to Jesus Christ. Backsliding is virtually impossible once you get to this point in your walk of faith. Remember, backsliding is <u>not</u> a dumb decision that you make or even a single sin (which we all still do because we are all sinners). Backsliding means you are going backwards in your faith. One of the reasons I wrote this book is to help believers move forward in your walk. That is the direction God wants us to go.

Anyway, our love for Christ does not depend on

how we feel or what kind of circumstances we are going through at the moment. This is life. We are supposed to have difficulties. The Word of God tells us that we will (John 16:33). Expect them and when they occur, persevere in them. Our faith will grow when we are put to the test of just how much we trust Jesus. By the way, you will have opportunities to trust Christ every single day. Make the most of them!

Being in the ministry means there is always somebody out there trying to knock you down so that they can feel built up. People who don't believe the way that you or I believe will always try to make you feel inferior to them. Let them. Be kind to them. Pray for them and love them. Isn't that what we are supposed to be doing? They are lost people doing what lost people do. They are exactly where we were at one point in our lives. Let's not beat the snot out of non-believers OR backsliders. Let's pray for them. Let's take them by the hand and walk with them during their time of confusion and searching. We have to do a better job of truly loving people.

I am saying all these things, because at times in my life, many years ago, I wished somebody would have done some of these things to me and for me. When Rebecca and I went through our difficult times, we didn't have anybody to lean on. The church that we were going to had simply vanished, and there was nobody there to help us along. You live by your mistakes. We have found that out the hard way too many times. So, one of the reasons I am writing this book is to help others know what they can do for Christ, but also a little about the cost that comes with serving Him. One of those costs is the negative way some people will treat you. Friends, we must be there for one another and encourage each other. We need to hold somebody's hand and have our own hands held at different times in our lives. Backsliding is not a fun place to be. But sometimes, going backwards reminds us what forward looks like and how best to get going back in the right direction.

If you are reading this right now and you are backsliding, my friend, stop and put down this book. Get on your knees and pray to God above to bring you back into His good and perfect will. This book can wait, but your business with God must be dealt with immediately. The great thing about our God is that He never sleeps and is always just right there waiting for you and I to come back to Him. How many times does He say in His word that He never leaves us, nor forsakes us (Hebrews 13:5)? The truth of the matter is that you and I are always the ones who depart from the path that God has designed for us. Pray right now and get your life squared back up with Him. You will be glad you did!!!

Easter Sunrise Service 2017.
Big Horn Mountains in the background.

CHAPTER 8

Acts 1:8 and People Differences

LET'S TALK ABOUT the different ways and the different kinds of people groups that you and I witness to. We need to discuss witnessing to your <u>family</u>, <u>friends</u>, <u>acquaintances</u>, and complete <u>strangers</u>. To better understand, we should take a look at those four groups in light of Acts 1:8. The Bible says, "But ye shall receive power, after that the Holy Ghost is come upon you: and ye shall be witnesses unto me both in Jerusalem, and in all Judaea, and in Samaria, and unto the uttermost part of the earth" (KJV).

Jerusalem

First, the Lord emphasized "Jerusalem." I like to compare this to your family. Your Jerusalem is where you live. It involves the people that you know the best. So, in my case, Jerusalem represents a small town in Wyoming called Greybull. That is where I live. According to Jesus, it is important to witness in your home town, even though it is quite challenging to do so (Mark 6:4). All home towns are tough, but the smaller the town the bigger the obstacles. People tend to know everything there is to know about you. In fact, they usually know what you did before you did it! Lol. But it must be done because Christ commands it AND it is a blessing and honor to serve the Lord in this way. Your next-door and across-town neighbors need to hear the Gospel of Jesus Christ just like your own family does. God did not place you in the next town over. He placed you exactly where you currently are.

Now, I totally understand the awkwardness and the uneasiness of witnessing to your own flesh and blood. We don't want to make people mad or make things weird between family. I get that. But my question then is this: How much do we actually *love* our family? Of course, we love them because they are "blood," but what about their soul? Do we not sense the importance of where their soul will end up for eternity? I am not saying that you shouldn't try to preserve the peace in your family. And yes, there is such a thing as being too aggressive when you are trying to witness. WE are the ones who *make* it awkward some of the time! But, we also <u>must</u>, from time to time try with due diligence to share our faith and values with our own family and closest friends.

I grew up in the West, but I have preached regularly in the South for many years. One of the things I have absolutely adored about some of the families we have ministered to, is that in a lot of cases, the entire family was saved: Grandmas, grandpas, aunts, uncles, brothers, sisters, cousins, nephews and nieces. What a testament to God's grace. It would absolutely blow my mind every time that these families could be so close with one another and have so much combined love for God. I was not used to seeing such a thing. I did not grow up with a family who grew and loved God together. I grew up living life and doing, more or less, whatever I wanted to do (and God wasn't usually part of the plan). This idea of having an entire family system that loved Jesus was beyond my comprehension. Later in life, though, I pleaded with God for that to be true of my own family. What a concept that your whole family could get together at Easter or Christmas and celebrate what that day actually meant. The question, then, becomes this: How determined will you be to help make this true of your family? Yes, it is God's grace and His power that transforms entire families. But He doesn't just do that randomly. Instead, He works through servants who are praying, obeying, and working hard to share their faith. Does that describe you?

You and I cannot change our past, but we can have some control over our future. So how do you actually tell one of your own family members that without Christ, they are dying and will burn in hell for all of eternity? Well, my suggestion is <u>not</u> to say that (at least not in so many words). Our families may be weird, but they are not dumb, and they don't want to be preached "at" every time they are around you. We simply must just love on our families every opportunity we get. While doing that, we have to constantly pray that God will appoint the time for a Gospel conversation. But when that happens (and it eventually will if that is what you are praying for), then you have to summon your courage and faithfully rise to the occasion.

We all know there is only one way to heaven, and we should be comfortable talking about that one Way. When your family member cracks open the door for you to have that conversation, then you have to be prayed up, and nudge the door open even further. You shouldn't kick down the door. But, neither can your family member afford for you to walk away. John 6:44 says, "No one can come to Me unless the Father who sent Me draws him; and I will raise him up at the last day" (NKJV). If God is drawing your family member to Him, at the right time, they will be ripe for the harvest. That's the good news. The bad news is that many

Christians value earthly harmony at family get-togethers more than reaping the souls that God has prepared for harvest.

Here's one of the issues: Your family knows you better than anyone else in the world. They know everything you ever did or didn't do. They also remember you from before you were "saved." Your character witness needs to be very strong. If you claim to have been changed by a relationship with Christ, then that change needs to have been very real and very obvious for everyone to see. Your own changed life after your conversion will be worth more to your family members than a thousand theology lessons. But if you are nothing but talk, strangers might not see that, but your family sure as heck will see you for what you are. Don't expect too many changes coming from your family, if the "change" you like to talk about never even took root in you!

My wife's mother got saved in 2017. She invited Rebecca and me over to her house to have a conversation. Mind you, up until this time we had both been a good witness to her for Christ. She started off the conversation by saying she did not know what we had, but she wanted it. She wanted what Rebecca and I had been exhibiting for all of those years around her. Rebecca explained to her own mother that she could absolutely have what we had—it was a relationship with Jesus Christ. She explained the gospel in a way that her mother could understand. In my wife's old house, in the dining room area, she got the privilege of leading her own mother to the Lord. It was a very special moment in Rebecca's life. She and I had been Christians for nearly 20 years before her mother was even remotely interested in understanding what it was that she was missing. God is so good like that.

Looking back, Rebecca's mother getting saved was glorious, obviously. However, it is a relationship that is backwards. In an ideal scenario, the father and mother would be the ones to lead their children to Christ. My friends, I don't have to tell you how messed up this world is. Rest assured, though, there is coming a day when everything will be in order. We must be ready for when that day comes. I have a saying that I give to churches all around the country that says, we must *be* ready, not just *getting* ready. We never know what is around the next corner of this life.

So, when it comes to witnessing to your family, the best thing to do is be prayed up before you start a conversation. Also, avoid confrontations whenever possible. Honestly, sometimes random strangers need someone to boldly speak the truth to them even if it is a tiny bit prickly. But I recommend, in most cases, against being confrontational with family. Why? Because you will usually get another chance (and another and another) to witness to family members. But if they are still hurt or angry about the last time, then they are not likely to be in the mood to listen the next time. There are exceptions to this rule, as you will see in the next paragraph. Also, confrontation is simply not persuasive. You can always intimidate someone else into agreeing with you through confrontation. But genuine Christian conversion has to do with the other person voluntarily deciding to trust and follow Jesus, not that the other person was beaten into submission, figuratively, and "lost" the argument.

If the spiritual conversation with a family member starts out bad, change the subject and move on. Wait until another day for when things are a bit calmer. But here's the exception. What if that day never comes? Let's say your father has a different belief than you. He is not saved. He is dying and most likely not going to leave the hospital. Now what do you do? Friend, in a case like this, lay it all on the line. If you choose to skirt around the subject, how do you think you will feel once your dad is gone? It will be crushing to you. You may or may not ever forgive yourself for your lack of boldness. What do you have to lose? Your time is running out. You have to act and pray for a death bed conversion right in front of your eyes. You must give it all you have so if he chooses to *not* accept the Gospel, you can at least know in your mind that you tried with all of your might to give him one final chance to be saved. *You* cannot save him, but God could. God is able even in the last moments of one's life to completely save a soul from spending eternity in hell.

I once heard a story about a man who was saved one night. In less than 10 minutes from him accepting Christ as Savior, the man was killed in a horrific automobile accident. Ten minutes before the accident, he was lost and going to hell. Ten minutes after being converted, he was standing in front of Jesus. Ten minutes isn't much time, as we all know; but our lives can be completely turned upside down in that amount of time. That was a deathbed conversion of another type. The man making the commitment to Christ never knew that he was so close to death. Praise God for those last 10 minutes! Oh, by the way, did I mention that someone took the time and made the effort to tell this man about Jesus? Sometimes, people are sick and obviously do not have much time left. In **all** other cases, we simply don't know how much more time on earth someone has. How stingy will you be with your Christian witness now that you know that some people will die in car wrecks (or countless other ways) within ten minutes of your opportunity to share with them how they can have everlasting life?

So, when speaking to your family, be diligent. Be humble. Own up to all the wrong things that they are almost certainly going to bring up about you. It's okay. That is who you once *were*. Share with them 2 Corinthians 5:17: "Therefore, if anyone is in Christ, he is a new creation; old things have passed away; behold, all things have become new" (NKJV). Your *old* self is no longer a part of the everyday picture. Yes, you *used* to do and say those things that a family member might accuse you of. Yes, of course, that *was* you. But praise God, you have been changed. You have been sealed. You have begun a brand-new life in Christ. Explain it to them, along with the hope that they can experience that same transformation too.

But we all know that actions speak louder than words. Rather than *telling* them, *show* them. If I *tell* you that I am a mechanic, but you never see me fix a car, then maybe I'm not really a mechanic. But if I say I am one, and then I actually can and <u>do</u> fix cars, people are much more likely to believe me. Again, actions speak louder than words. Our lifestyle as Christians should be the exact same way. I don't want anybody to ever hear me say that I am a Christian, but then walk away thinking, *really?*

So, sharing the Gospel with your family, in my humble opinion, is definitely one of the hardest groups of people to share with. Be prayed up, watch for the right times and then faithfully sit down and try to have a gospel conversation with them. The Lord knows your heart (and theirs). Be thankful if and when your family gives you the opportunity to finally share what is on your mind. It is truly a blessing when God uses you to reach your very own family with the truth.

Judea

Secondly, you can think about Judaea as representing your friends. These are going to be people that you know, trust, and enjoy being around for the most part. Your friends know you in a different kind of way than your family. Your closest friends *could* even know at least a few things that your family doesn't even know. You might say that your friends know the "crazy" part of you. By God's grace, you are now saved, and one would think that you should want to tell your buddies. Here is how that often goes. After they initially stare at you with their mouths dropped open, they might roll their eyes. They might laugh out loud. They might rant for several minutes against religion, past negative church experiences, or even God himself. Your news is *not* what they were expecting to hear when you first opened your mouth. Get ready for a total lack of support. This is a very typical way that friends respond. It's totally fine, though. They are responding like lost people. There was probably a time, maybe not even all that long ago, when you might have responded in the exact same way. Press on. Keep sharing with them. Just like with your family, continue to live out your faith in front of them.

Their reaction will likely continue for a little while. But then, one of three things typically happen. First, and the best thing, is that your friends will follow suit and get saved. That is one of the most awesome experiences that we can have. You loved your friends enough to tell them about Jesus Christ. In turn, they will love you now for the rest of your life. There will be a bond between you that you never had before. It is an extremely strong bond, and is built on something much more durable than hunting, fishing, recreation, and hobbies.

There is power in numbers. Look at what God says in Ecclesiastes 4:9: "Two are better than one, because they have a good reward for their labor" (NKJV). Then verse 12 says, "...and a threefold cord is not quickly broken" (NKJV). Keep sharing your faith with your friends.

Wouldn't it be nice to have an army of friends who

are believers? Think about what you could accomplish with so many Christian friends. That should continue to motivate you to share with as many buddies as you can. You are their friend. Your salvation is <u>not</u> a "private" matter, as it is characterized by so many people these days. God has saved you for the PUBLIC good!

I would also like to point out that you have a circle of friends that other people cannot easily break into. But, please know that God has you right where He wants you. There is a reason you have remained friends with certain people over the years. It is entirely likely that you will be able to share the Gospel with people who nobody else will ever get the chance to. It is always very meaningful to fulfill a mission that only *you* can do. Whatever the case, just know that your friends are a key part of your mission field. Don't be embarrassed or ashamed. Christ was not embarrassed or ashamed when He laid down His life for you. He willingly went to the cross for you and for me and for your *friends*. Let us willingly share our faith with all of our friends, whether they accept it or not.

Secondly, what could happen is that your friends eventually get fed up with your newfound faith and y'all will simply have to agree to disagree. At this point, it is kind of like they have (seemingly) won the game. They value your friendship, but they are not willing to hear about this Jesus anymore. You can still remain friends with people like this. I have one atheist friend who at certain times will comment on one of my social media posts. You don't have to look very far into this person to see that he does not believe in Christ. One day, after a remark he had made, I simply said, "Marcus (Yes, that is his real name and Yes, I have his permission to talk about him in this book.), I want you to know that every time God lays you on my heart, I pray for you to someday be saved." His answer astonished me. He said, "Thank you. I always appreciate the prayers and *if* your God is real, I want to know that as well someday." WOW! I don't have to tell you I was blown away – an atheist thanking me for a prayer. It made me realize that just because we do not believe the same things, it doesn't have to change the way that I act toward him. My job is not to save anybody or to judge anybody. My job is to be faithful and obedient to God and walk through every single witnessing door He opens. My friend, that is your job as well. We have no saving grace to offer anybody, yet our conversations with people are a very important piece of how God works to reach people with his love.

So, no matter the situation, just understand that it is God who chooses to work through us in order to reach people in a saving way. Once you become a Christian, you have to live to help others become Christians as well. Be determined to grow spiritually every day and continue to fall deeper in love with the Lord Jesus Christ. Keep on learning. Keep on maturing. Exercise your faith, just like a muscle, so that it can get bigger and stronger. Remember my friend Rhyan from the last chapter? It took witnessing to him for nearly 10 years before he got saved. It is amazing how often God rewards perseverance. Keep up the great work!

Thirdly, and by far the worst thing that can happen when you try and share your faith with one of your friends, is the potential of losing them altogether. But to what lengths would you go to see your friend saved? Do you love your friend enough to share the only way to heaven, or do you *not* love them quite that much? Do you value their friendship more than their salvation? If you tell them about Christ, they *might* hate you for it and not want to be your friend anymore. But also, if you tell them about Christ, they might repent immediately and call on the name of the Lord to be saved.

Should you or should you not "risk" the friendship in order to make sure your friend hears the Gospel? We all know the right answer, but it is still a hard question to think about. I have been there on both sides. Many years back, I had a great friend. We hunted and fished together and always had a great time. My friend and I had very different beliefs. He was a Mormon and I was a Christian. I had prayed and asked God if I should try and share with him the differences between the two. By the way, in case you are not sure about this, there are eternal differences between the two belief systems. After much prayer I called him one day and basically said, "Dude I have something on my mind. We have two totally different beliefs. We both know that. If I was to print out some differences between what I believe and what you believe, would you read them and tell me your honest opinions?" He said, "Sure I will do that." I fervently prayed and begged God for the truth to finally set this man free.

Unfortunately, that was the last phone call we ever had (so far). He went on social media and promptly bashed the snot out of me. He tried to make me out to be the bad guy who was "better" than him. I had a choice to make. Either, I could not share with him and feel guilty about that or I could share with him and run the risk that he would do exactly what he ended up doing. It's hard to believe that just speaking the truth and sharing your faith with one of your closest friends would result in them leaving your life. It truly broke my heart. That was nearly eight years ago, at the time of this writing, and we have yet to speak another word.

Since then, this man has moved several hundred

miles away. But there are times that he still comes to my mind and I have to ask myself whether or not I did the right thing. In my opinion, here's how you have to answer that question. Do I love my friends enough to take the risk of them shutting me out of their life for the rest of our days? My hope, obviously, was that he would have read through the material and realized that he was not saved and was following a false god. Then, I hoped he would have called me and said, "thank you, thank you, thank you! Because you loved me enough to share the differences, I got saved! I now know that I will spend my eternity in heaven." Okay, maybe that was a little naïve, but that was the gist of what I secretly expected. Needless to say, it did not happen that way.

So, was it worth it? I surely didn't like losing one of my top five best friends, but my conscience was clear. I was faithful to God. But what if I had made the opposite decision? What if you decide not to tell your best friend in the world that if they don't accept Jesus Christ as their Lord and Savior, they will not spend eternity in heaven, but in hell below? I heard a preacher somewhere say it like this: Suppose you get to heaven and before you can enter, you have to take a shoebox full of each person's blood that you did not share with (but you could have) and pour it out on the ground, knowing that person will never be in heaven. I'm sure that won't be how it is, but what if it was? It is painful and disturbing to me just to type it!

If we disobey God's Word on evangelizing all because we don't want to lose a friend, then you <u>contribute</u> to that other person remaining in their current state. What if someone spends their whole life thinking that they are saved, but if they could hear you explain the biblical doctrine of original sin, they would know they are not saved? My friend, when we stay silent, it is shame on us. Are you the kind of friend that would let this happen? If you are like me, if I am absolutely wrong on something, I want to know. Will I be upset when someone sets me straight? Perhaps, but the Bible says in John 8:32, "And ye shall know the truth, and the truth shall make you free" (KJV). Likewise, spiritual truth will set your friends free once they understand the eternal cost of sin and the redemption that comes through Christ. And speaking of eternity, they will be eternally grateful for your friendship and courage. Don't base your course of action on a *hunch* about how your friends *might* respond to you sharing your faith. Rather, be bold in the Lord, and put the ball in the other person's court.

But my whole take on this is if I have the keys to heaven and I choose to *not* give them to every person that I come in contact with, then that is my bad. I don't want to be guilty of this. I want to love people in such a way that they see their eternal status as way more important than their earthly status. And yes, that includes friends. I pray for my Mormon friend as often as I think about him. I still pray that God will put somebody new in his path who will share the truth with him again. Maybe the next time he hears it, he will respond differently. God is a God of second chances, so there is good reason to hope.

By the way, there is nothing easy about this. However, if I know that a friend of mine is following a false god, then in my heart, I cannot justify an earthly relationship being more important than a heavenly one. Our earthly life is very temporary. It lasts 70, 80, or maybe even 90-plus years. But our time spent in heaven or hell will last infinity times infinity times infinity. My friend, you could provide the one conversation that leads to their eternal status being changed. Pray it up, as I have said many times in this book, and brace yourself for whichever way the conversation may go. Just be aware of how much you love or don't love this friend. That will dictate which way that this friendship may go. If it goes south, it will sting. But at least you will sleep at night knowing that you did your best to offer heaven to your friend.

Samaria

Your acquaintances can be associated with Samaria. These are people that you kind of know or who you have contact with once in a while. You can be friends with them, but your paths don't really cross all that often. The question you have to ask yourself is, "Won't they be spending eternity somewhere too?" Do we go the extra mile for family and friends, but then turn away from our acquaintances? Does their eternity mean anything to you? Being a Christian means that *everybody's* eternity should mean something to us. Just because you don't visit with this person very often, doesn't mean you shouldn't care about their soul. You don't have to know somebody intimately well in order to care about them. In fact, God says we are to love and care about our enemies and even total strangers (Romans 12:14-21; Hebrews 13:2).

If you are going to share the gospel with a person who you don't know all that closely, what do you have to lose? The answer is *nothing*. At least I can understand some of the thoughts we often have before witnessing to family and friends. But casual acquaintances? Just be yourself and share the greatest news ever given to mankind. My experience is that they are usually kind enough to at least hear you out. They won't feel compelled to believe just because you believe (which is good). And they also will not feel like if they don't believe that you are going to become any less to them than you already are (also good). Of course, the goal should usually be to move acquaintances into the "friend" column over time. But while they are mere acquaintances, there is no real bond between the two of you. This removes some of the potential messiness that exists with family and close friends. So, don't be afraid to be extremely bold.

But let's say that you begin a spiritual conversation with him or her and they are astounded. They look at you and say they never knew that about you. To be honest, that should be a little embarrassing that we kept or hid that part of our life from anybody. From personal experience, though, I can tell you that they are just as likely to say, "You know I have been thinking about this for a long time. I just didn't know for sure. But you say *you* are a believer and that *you* have trusted Christ for your salvation?" You say "yes," of course. But then you need to say this: "I am sorry that I never shared this with you before. And just because we are not close does not mean that I don't care about where you will spend your eternity. Let's talk."

Imagine if that person gets saved because you were willing and bold enough to share with them. My guess is that relationship was just moved from *acquaintance* to *pretty good friend*, and soon-to-be *very good friend*. Why? Because they are going to need you like they didn't need you before. You are now going to move into a disciple-maker kind of role. That, my friends, is a good thing. That means that you communicated the gospel to this person in an effective manner. When presented with the gospel, they acknowledged and received it, repented of their sins, and were saved. That is always a great thing and you can feel blessed that God used you to reach that other person. Trust me when I say that many Christians ignore the Samaritans in their lives.

To the end of the earth

So, we know that Acts 1:8 tells us to be witnesses in Jerusalem, Judea, Samaria, and to the uttermost parts of the earth. I hope it made sense as we talked about family, friends, and acquaintances. Now we need to think about what Christ meant when He said we are to bear witness to him to the uttermost parts of the world. We need to discuss how to share the gospel with complete strangers. Why? Because our bubbles get much too small sometimes. We have our family and a handful of close friends. But that is, what, a dozen people? Two dozen? Far fewer? In a world of BILLIONS, practically everyone is a stranger.

You are probably thinking to yourself, "I cannot share the gospel with people I do not know." Or, "I don't really get out that much and so I don't really get any opportunities." Since I am not in the pulpit at this moment, I believe I have the right to say "bull." Whoa preacher. How can you say that? The answer is very easy. It's called math. You are literally surrounded by strangers every day of your life. Some move out while others move in to take their place.

In just this past week, how many of us pumped gas at a gas station? How many of us ate out at a restaurant? How many of us went to a grocery store? Those are only three places. In those three places, how many times did we actually converse with absolute strangers? You may <u>not</u> have, but none of us should pretend that we didn't have the opportunity.

Men especially, how many times did we talk to somebody this week about the weather, or the game, or hunting or fishing? My best guestimate is several times plus four. We're men. We can typically talk to just about anybody, because men have a script with other men that makes conversation easy. The script includes, among a few other things, exactly what I just mentioned: weather, sports, hunting, and fishing. So, if you are thinking that you just can't talk to complete strangers, you and I both know that isn't true. You like-ly avoid having *spiritual* conversations with strangers. That I understand, but that is what we need to learn to do. Ladies, the same is true for you. If you can talk for hours with your best friend about any topic under the sun, then you are certainly *able* to talk to strangers. You might avoid it. It may make you anxious. It's possible that you don't currently enjoy talking with strangers. But you ARE able to do it, and strangers need Jesus!

If we are keeping Acts 1:8 in our minds, then we truly don't have any reasons to avoid spreading the gospel at any time or with any person. Over the last decade, Rebecca and I have been to countless rodeos and fairs to share the gospel with the attendees (and contestants!). This is not bragging, but we have helped share the gospel tens of thousands of times with thou-sands of people praying to receive Christ all over this great nation. We have trained folks how to do the same (see Chapter 4). Obviously, most of these thousands of people were complete strangers to us. But we didn't let that stop us. Again, there are things that make witness-ing to strangers even easier than witnessing to family and friends. You can do this!

So, start off with some pleasantries. "Hi. My name is James from Wyoming. What's been going on with you?" They, in return, will at least tell you their name and where they are from. In a gospel-sharing booth scenario, we usually ask them for three minutes of their time. Three minutes is obviously not very long, so you have to really focus on what is most important for that other person to hear. If you have learned to share your faith story, then make sure you have time built into it to also share the actual gospel message. Remember that your salvation story, even though it is a wonderful testament to God's grace, has no saving effect whatsoever for anyone else. Only a personal response of faith in Jesus Christ can save a lost person.

Although I have trained thousands of folks to share their faith story and then the Gospel, personally, I rarely use my "story" anymore. I have found that if I just get to the Gospel and spend the majority of my time talking about Jesus Christ (rather than me), then I feel like I have done a better job of managing my three-minute time slot. I will occasionally use bits and pieces of my story to help draw the net, but for the most part, I really just stick to the Gospel. That is truly the best thing any of us can offer to a lost person! The Gospel changes people's lives. I know this to be true because this cowboy from Wyoming is writing a book that has been inspired by the saving grace of our Lord and Savior Jesus Christ. It will absolutely change your life and everything about it. You will never be the same person again once you have a true encounter with the Living God, Jesus Christ. Did I mention that Jesus Christ ought to be the focus when we are witnessing?

I don't think anybody can truly meet with Christ and come away the same person. Therefore, our job is really simple: introduce people to Jesus. If you truly meet Him or if He truly meets you and you walk away unchanged, I would say your wood is wet. Nobody in their right mind could have an encounter with God and not see the power and the majesty that is before them.

Let me share a story about my good friend and brother in Christ, Dean Cook. Dean is the pastor of Cross Brand Cowboy Church in Sylvarena, Mississippi. He and his lovely wife were travelling one summer. They stopped at a rest area along the interstate. They both went into their respective restrooms. My buddy Dean came out first and noticed two workers working on the grounds of the rest area. He started talking to them about the weather and how nice the place looked and just made some small chit chat. His wife came out and they both walked back to their vehicle. He turned the car on and sat there for a moment. He then told his wife, "Baby, I have to go back over to those workers." He approached the two men and said, "Fellas, I owe you an apology." As you can imagine, they were intrigued as to what he would have to be sorry for.

My buddy went on to tell them that he came over and talked about just regular old conversation stuff. Truly, it was all just meaningless from an eternal perspective. Then he said, "But I have neglected to tell you about my Jesus. It is shame on me for not mentioning to you the greatest name of all time. My Jesus is really all I need to be talking about." So, he shared the Gospel with both men who were working and neither of them were saved. My friend Dean led both of those men to the Lord at a rest area along the interstate.

He was embarrassed that he didn't share with them sooner. But the Holy Spirit gave him a conviction before it was too late and my buddy responded to that conviction. I am thankful and so were the two men that his conviction made him get back out of his vehicle and walk back over and first, *apologize* for not sharing the Gospel. Then he made it right by *sharing* the Gospel. Wow!!!! How many of us would have simply missed out on that blessing because of our disobedience to Christ? My guess is, and this is just a guess, many if not most of the readers of this book.

I am just writing as honestly as I can. Thankfully, Dean got the blessing and two men received eternal life. He responded to the Spirit's conviction and then he went and shared. We have much to learn from this story. You and I will miss out on countless blessings if we do not learn to become more faithful and obedient to God. He is faithful to provide the opportunities, but we will have to step out of our comfort zones if we want to receive the blessings.

One more thing that I truly love about this story is that it teaches us that we can mess up, realize our mess up, and then turn around and right the wrong. Dean did a great thing. I hope that story will inspire millions of the rest of us to always be thinking about the right thing to do, even when sometimes we do not initially get the right thing done.

I am reminded as well of when Paul spoke about not doing what he wanted to do and doing what he didn't want to do. Romans 7:15-25 says:

I do not understand what I do. For what I want to do I do not do, but what I hate I do. And if I do what I do not want to do, I agree that the law is good. As it is, it is no longer I myself who do it, but it is sin living in me. For I know that good itself does not dwell in me, that is, in my sinful nature. For I have the desire to do what is good, but I cannot carry it out. For I do not do the good I want to do, but the evil I do not want to do—this I keep on doing. Now if I do what I do not want to do, it is no longer I who do it, but it is sin living in me that does it. So I find this law at work: Although I want to do good, evil is right there with me. For in my inner being I delight in God's law; but I see another law at work in me, waging war against the law of my mind and making me a prisoner of the law of sin at work within me. What a wretched man I am! Who will rescue me from this body that is subject to death? Thanks be to God, who delivers me through Jesus Christ our Lord! (NIV)

When you read that text, there are a lot of to-do's and not-to-dos. But there is hope. Paul, who was arguably the greatest missionary ever is showing us his own struggles. He wants to do good but doesn't always get the job done. Referring back to my friend Dean, he was immediately convicted of not doing what he should have done. But again, the difference between Dean and most others, is that Dean acted upon his conviction. This is where all of us should strive to get to. I want my disobedience to lead to conviction resulting in repentance and ultimately me taking the actions that God was leading me to do all along. Yes, it would be much easier to just always make the right decisions at first. However, it is better to *eventually* do what is right than to not do the right thing at all. The more we continue to grow and mature in the Lord, the less conviction it will take for us to obey God. This is a good thing and it pleases God greatly when we are quick to obey.

That is also what it looks like when we give up the sippy cup and start to eat the solids of the Bible. The knowledge and the truths that we continue to learn and apply will help us to grow and become a stronger and more faithful follower of the Lord. Do not give up just because you aren't "there" yet. I am not writing this book to congratulate awesome Christians nearly as much as I am writing to help Christians to be better-equipped to effectively serve Christ. The growth and health of the church depends on all of us learning, maturing, responding to the Spirit's conviction, and getting out of our comfort zone in order to share the Gospel with everyone we come into contact with. Again, you can do this!

CHAPTER **9**

How Saved Is 97 Percent?

IN THIS CHAPTER, I want to address some of the faulty thinking that prevents many people from being saved. I do not mean to go overboard with theology. Rather, I just want to try and provide some answers for you so that you can respond to people when they raise some common objections or when they make faulty arguments. For example…

How do you witness to somebody who says they are 97% saved? This happens more often that you might think. I suppose that some people say it that way because they are trying to be humble and not want to suggest that they are, by gosh, 1,000 percent positive that they are going to heaven when they die. But let's just take people at their word for a moment. Being 97% saved equates to being 3% lost. We all know (I hope by now) that lost people do not go to heaven.

Only saved folks go to heaven. This is super basic but super important at the same time. Do not congratulate someone for scoring themselves so "high." The truth is that there is no such thing as being 97% saved. You are either saved or you are not. Those are the only two choices. And anyone who gives a percentage on their salvation needs to be told lovingly but bluntly that their answer doesn't make any sense.

I was sharing the Gospel one time with a teenage boy. I started telling him about Jesus. He interrupted and said, "Sir, I am saved." I said, "Great. How saved are you?" He said, with a great big smile, "I am about 97% saved." So, I looked at him with a great big smile and said, "So you are telling me that you are 3% lost?" He wasn't smiling after that. We are so apt to say we are saved even if we aren't truly saved. This young man thought he had it all together; well, all but about 3%. We cannot be saved until we repent and surrender 100% to Jesus, at which time He 100% saves us.

At one time in my life, I thought in a similar way. I gave Jesus what I felt He could handle—about 90% of my affairs. What kind of an idiot thinks God can only handle a fraction of His business? Me! I was that idiot! And since I was badly mistaken about who God really was (and the power He really had) it kept me from surrendering completely to Him. Praise the Eternal

Father that 20-plus years ago, I gave Him <u>all</u> of me. He now has all of the good, the bad and the ugly things of James. I am way less than 100% perfect, but by God's grace, I am 100% saved and 100% sure about that salvation.

When witnessing to the masses, I typically hear some of the same things over and over. I am a *pretty* good person. I have never *killed* anyone before. I am a good and moral person. If God can't accept me for who I am, then I am not interested in Him. How can a good God let children starve and die? How can a good God allow bad things to happen? Truly the list of things people say can go on and on and on.

First off, remind people that God doesn't compare us to any other human being; therefore, we shouldn't be comparing ourselves to others either. It is a very popular ploy by lost people. Because, yes, most people are "better" than Adolf Hitler. But we can be "better" than Hitler in terms of the number of people we have murdered or the world wars we have started, while still being just as bad as Hitler spiritually. The point is that Hitler is not the standard anyway; God is the standard. God does not use imperfect, earthly ways to judge people. He uses a perfect, heavenly standard. Romans 3:23 makes it clear that we have ALL sinned and fall short of the glory of God. We have all failed and at times continue to fail. Frantically trying to come up with an example of someone who is "worse" than us is not how this thing works. When you are witnessing, it is more than okay to correct peoples' faulty thinking about this.

I love it when people say, "I am a pretty good person." Tell me then, why would Jesus have to die on the cross in the manner in which He did, if all we had to do was be a pretty good person? It's more than being a pretty good person. We cannot save ourselves. Salvation is a gift from God. The Bible says, "For by grace are ye saved through faith; and that not of yourselves: it is the gift of God: not of works, lest any man should boast" (Ephesians 2:8-9, KJV). You cannot earn it. It is not up to you to be good enough (because there's no such thing). Your salvation is an entirely free gift given to you from God above. You either accept it or reject it. You cannot be *almost* saved. You are either saved or not saved. You are either in or out. Again, be as gentle as you like, but don't let someone walk away from the conversation still clinging to a blatantly wrong position.

Here is an off the wall kind of illustration I gave in a sermon one time about witnessing to someone who is 97% saved. If I made you a beautiful looking chocolate cake, would you eat it? Yes, right? But what would you do if you had a piece of it on your fork and had it almost to your mouth and I said, "Hey I just wanted you to know that I added only 3% dog poop to the ingredients?" You are going to gag and throw it out. Right? You will most likely not be very happy with me. But in my defense, I am going to say that there is only 3% in it. You, my friend, just told me that you were 97% saved which means what about your other 3%? I am telling you that chocolate cake is 97% going to be great, but you are not going to be willing to eat it. Do you see the comparison? You are saying one thing but then showing another, because 3% is still 3%. Nobody in their right mind would ever eat a chocolate cake like that. It is the truth for our salvation as well. Nobody can be 97% saved and still expect to go to heaven. Why? Because God thinks about the same of our sin as you do about the dog poop. Most of the cake is great, but... Most of our life might be pretty moral, but...

God is not asking any of us to be *mostly* saved. He requires us to be saved, in fact, 100% saved. Can you now start to understand why Christ did what only Christ could do? Being good enough is not nearly enough. In the ministry world, we call it the "good ole boy" syndrome. Good ole boys exist all over this great country. These are people who don't cheat or lie. Maybe they don't drink or smoke. Maybe they obey the law, work hard, and never say a bad word about anybody. But being a "good" ole boy does not get you to heaven. Only having your sin debt cancelled by the blood of Christ does.

We were in a Bible Study one time talking about salvation. A man told us that a neighbor had broken one of his legs. This was during haying season. Another neighbor heard about it and brought his haying machinery over and cut and baled this man's hay. The man in the Bible Study thought that good deed was enough to get to heaven. I explained that was a great thing and most likely the right thing to do, but doing the "right" thing is not enough to get anybody to heaven either. If all we had to do was the right thing every time, then why would Christ have to die the way He did on the cross? The man pondered this for a while and then agreed that it had to be more than just good works (Ephesians 2:8-9).

How about the person who says I am going to heaven because I have never killed anyone? My question to him would be, "Are you sure? Are you sure you have never killed anybody?" In 1 John 3:15 it says, "Anyone who hates a brother or sister is a murderer, and you know that no murderer has eternal life residing in him" (NIV). You could then say something like: "I will agree with you that I have not killed anybody either, but the Bible, God's inerrant Word, gives us the guidelines (and definitions). Jesus Christ himself says that hating somebody is the same as murder (Matthew 5:21-22). Now that we know that, it puts each of us into a different category. To be honest with people, the simple fact is there's probably not too many people alive who have not hated at least one person or at least one time in their life. It gets worse.

Maybe someone will tell you, "I have never cheated on my spouse." You can say, "That's great. Neither have I, at least in the way you mean it." But then you have to take that person back to the Bible and see what God actually has to say about that. Matthew 5:28 reads, "But I tell you that anyone who looks at a woman lustfully has already committed adultery with her in his heart" (NIV). Friends, that incriminates just about every single one of us! I would be shocked if there is a single person reading this book who hasn't committed this sin. Matthew 5:28, obviously, applies to women as well. But can a solitary man honestly say that when a pretty woman walked by, at SOME point in your life, you didn't have thoughts that you shouldn't have had? One, there are many people out there who will try to sell that. And two, they will suggest that being faithful to their spouse ought to give them the credit they need to get to heaven. Again, that isn't how it works, and you will have to be the one to help correct peoples' faulty thinking.

We think differently than the Lord Jesus Christ. Isaiah 55:8 says, "For my thoughts are not your thoughts, neither are your ways my ways,' declares the Lord" (NIV). To be honest, I am grateful that God and I do not think alike. You see, we try to compare ourselves and our ways to somebody who is less than us or less perfect than us. That is easy to do. It always makes us look good. If it didn't, we wouldn't have chosen that comparison. But God has already given us the ways to compare our holiness to His.

If we compare ourselves to Hitler, we are good. But my friend, Hitler is not your Savior. What happens when you compare yourself to the God of the universe, the Creator of all creation? Now how do you sit? Not very well and neither do I. That is why God is God and we must play by His rules. This whole world is His, not ours. God is the boss and He says that He will judge humankind using Christ as the standard (not Hitler, not your neighbor, not some criminal on TV, and not anyone else). The average lost person struggles with this simple truth. They are busy comparing their righteousness to others, and they conveniently pick the worst of the worst to compare themselves to. But God compares us to the One who is perfectly righteous, with no sin whatsoever—Jesus Christ.

You don't have to make sure every person you meet has flawless theology, but you must help others get these unbiblical ways of thinking out of their minds. The truth is that each one of us is a sinner, and every sinner on the face of the earth needs a savior. The only Savior who can save my soul or your soul is Jesus Christ. Period!! Do not be afraid to tell people that. Our salvation is found in no one else (Acts 4:12). Praise the Lord (!) that He has told us these things plainly beforehand. There is no reason for anyone to be confused. So, just share the plain, scriptural truth with people. Their eternal destiny depends on it.

Another common objection to God and Christianity is the question on many peoples' minds: Why do bad things happen to good people or why is there so much evil in the world? You can't swing a dead cat without hitting someone who has rejected Christ on the basis of these questions. The answer you need to give is one little three-letter word – sin. I've looked up the definition in the dictionary before and it seems to usually mention that sin is an immoral act considered to be a violation of divine law. That's not a terrible definition. In a biblical sense, sin is what keeps you and I from the one, true, perfect and holy God. After the fall of Adam and Eve (Genesis 3), we have since been under it. The fall will someday be reversed, but not in this world. So, everything about this current world in which you and I live is under sin and under the fall. God has allowed this since the beginning. Why do you think He had to have His son Jesus in place to cover our sins so that we may have the opportunity to get to Heaven? Because we are "fallen" and need to have our sins forgiven, and this cannot happen without divine help.

The sin that was committed in the garden, did not take God by surprise. God is never surprised by what He created. He knows all things, all the time. There will come a day when we will not be living under sin anymore. I would hope that each reader longs for that day. Revelation 21:1-4 reads like this:

> And I saw a new heaven and a new earth: for the first heaven and the first earth were passed away; and there was no more sea. And I John saw the holy city, new Jerusalem, coming down from God out of heaven, prepared as a bride adorned for her husband. And I heard a great voice out of heaven saying, Behold, the tabernacle of God is with men, and he will dwell with them, and they shall be his people, and God himself shall be with them, and be their God. And God shall

wipe away all tears from their eyes; and there shall be no more death, neither sorrow, nor crying, neither shall there be any more pain: for the former things are passed away. (KJV)

Our perfect place is coming someday but not yet. God has had all of this planned and prepared for those who have put their faith and trust in Him. All things will be made new someday. For us, who have wept, and have had sorrow, and have lived a life of pain, it says there will be no more. No more imperfections, just holiness for the rest of eternity. No more sin, just paradise for all of eternity. You and I are living under the fall right now, but someday we will be living in paradise. Hope is a powerful thing. The lost people you get to talk with will be very interested in hearing the truth about a better future. Because many people's lives are a constant struggle here in this world. You are offering them a chance to have their tears wiped away forever. But that opportunity comes only through Christ. But God is putting you in the position to offer genuine hope to that person. Trust the Holy Spirit's guidance in that moment and boldly offer Jesus as the final solution to peoples' struggles.

If people need further teaching on this matter, you can say that everything that we see, or smell, or touch, or can eat, or hear as of now is under the fall. We look at the rainbow in the sky, and marvel at how pretty it is. Wait until we see those colors in a perfect world. Think about your favorite food (now you're probably hungry!). Wait until you eat that food in heaven above where there is no sin. Our lives in Christ will only get better as time goes by, or maybe I should say, when there is no more time or space, meaning heaven some-day. All things will be better when we are standing with our Savior, Jesus Christ in heaven. This is what all believers get to look forward to. And this is a powerful argument for people to give up the pitiful things of this world and instead put their trust in the Lord who has prepared a perfect paradise for everyone who would simply believe on the Name of the Lord Jesus Christ.

The key to understanding why bad things happen in this life is sin. We come by it naturally, and we often bring it upon ourselves by the choices we make. Every person reading this book (and everyone not reading it) has a sin nature. We must continue to make ourselves aware of it, and intentionally try to stay on top of it each day.

Just because we have a sin nature does not give us a license to continue to live in our sin. When we do sin, the Holy Spirit does a great job convicting us almost immediately. After that, we have a choice to make. Do we ask for forgiveness or do we just keep on sinning? Truly, if we are saved and are living like we are saved, we will repent right then and there and move on. Yes, Christians sin, but please don't think you can live a habitual lifestyle of sinning. Also, please don't think you can willfully disobey God and continue to live "for" Him. It simply doesn't work like that.

Remember, when you got saved, your old ways were meant to go away. You are no longer that old self; you are a brand-new creation in Jesus Christ (2 Corinthians 5:17). Why would anybody want to continue to live for the old self when we have a brand-new life in Christ Jesus? Jesus made the way, so let us live our lives according to His good and perfect will and not our own. Why are there so many problems in the world? Because there is so much sin in the world. Who has offered a way for the problems of sin to be removed and reversed? The answer is God through Christ. That is a message that still sells, even 2,000 years after the resurrection. Keep on preaching Jesus to a lost and dying world. All of creation needs it!

CHAPTER 10

Counting the Costs

SIT BACK FOR a moment and try to calculate what it has cost you for being a Christian or for sharing the Gospel. It may sound strange to hear this, but I sincerely hope that it has cost you, at least, *something*! Because, costs are inevitable when you start to follow or share Christ. One must first come to terms that it will cost them something, or else your Christian walk will be phony. That makes this one of the first tests of whether your faith is even real or not. Christ sacrificed His <u>life</u> for us. Are we even willing to be called a bad name for Him? Are we willing to have a door slammed in our face for Him? If not, then our faith is pretty sad. Right? Paying some sort of price for following Jesus is a foregone guarantee. In fact, Jesus flat-out said that He is sending us out as lambs among wolves (Luke 10:3). So, this aspect of following Christ is non-negotiable. We don't get to make the rules about whether Christianity costs anything. It does.

One thing is for sure when we are talking about legitimate followers of Christ or Christians who regularly share the Gospel. At some point in our lives, we will lose relationships, dreams, material things and/or perhaps even our lives. It is commonly thought that at least 10 out of the 12 original disciples lost their lives for their continued faith in Christ. I shared earlier in this book what it was like to have lost a great friend. It is still difficult to talk about, but I do have peace that I gave it my all to lead this man to Christ. Living for Jesus is not always easy. Galatians 5:24 says, "And those who belong to Christ Jesus have crucified the flesh with its passions and desires" (ESV). In other words, your flesh and blood has been bought with the most precious blood ever given to anybody. When you get saved or got saved, you actually transfer ownership of yourself to God. That means that furthering *His* kingdom and implementing *His* plans take priority over our own wants, wishes, and desires. Sometimes that means that we suffer some sort of loss, but it glorifies God, therefore, it is good.

It totally makes sense, when you really think about it, because you and I were made in His image anyway. If you want to live for Christ, then Christ must be at the head of your life. Matthew 16:24-25 reads like this, "Then Jesus told His disciples, 'If anyone would come after me, let him deny himself and take up his cross and follow me. For whoever would save his life will lose it, but whoever loses his life for my sake will find it'" (ESV). Yes, there will be costs and we must be able to count them. But will it be worth it? Heaven verses hell, life verses death, complete togetherness with God verses eternal separation; with every breath in my body, I say to you it will be worth it. I guarantee nobody is going to want to miss it, once they understand the truth.

I have said this a thousand times in the past when witnessing to people. There will be some folks who will miss heaven by 12 inches. How do you figure, the other person often asks? There are a lot of folks who have knowledge of Jesus and what He did for us, but have never been able to get the knowledge from their *head* to their *heart*. If all we have is knowledge when we die, then we will suffer that eternal separation for all of eternity. I can attest to this since I was saved a little bit later in life. I *knew* who God was. I *knew* who Jesus was. I had even called on their names and prayed to "them." I had the *knowledge* but I had no relationship at all. I had never repented of my sins and I had never called on Jesus to be my Lord and Savior.

How about another kind of cost? I was preaching in Mississippi a few years back and some good folks had taken us out to eat at a seafood restaurant. Like Rebecca and I do at all restaurants, I asked the waitress if there was any specific way that we could pray for her. She explained her prayer requests. We prayed with her, and then I asked her if they were open on Sundays? She said, "We used to be, but not anymore." I inquired further. She said, "Well, there is the owner right over there. You can go and visit with him." As you probably know by now, I am not a very shy person, so I got up and went over and introduced myself to the owner.

He was a very pleasant man. I asked him why he wasn't open on Sundays anymore. He said, "Well, the Lord dealt with me about this. By staying open on Sundays, I realized I might have been the reason some of my employees were not going to church. I was convicted, so I told the Lord I would honor Him by closing my business on Sundays." I told him I thought that was an amazing testimony. I dug just a little deeper. I asked him if he knew what it cost him financially to close his business on Sundays. He said, "Yes sir. It costs me a million dollars, gross, every year to be closed on Sundays." Wow! Most of us can barely conceive a number like that. Right?

Can you imagine loving Christ so much that you would give up making a million dollars per year? Can you imagine how much spiritual peace you and I would have if we listened to God about our finances? Can you imagine what it is like to live fully within the will of God? Can you imagine what that peace feels like that transcends all of our human understanding? I shook that man's hand and I was grateful to have met him. I prayed for him to continue to be blessed and for him to continue to be faithful to Almighty God. It wasn't about the money to him; it was about bringing honor and glory to God. I want that same thing today (and every day for the rest of my life). I want the integrity that says, "Lord, I may not understand it, but I will honor you in all of my ways, even if it costs a million dollars."

I have never forgotten that man or his story. The costs of following Christ can be astronomical. But our God is worth it. Whether it's a million-dollar loss, a special relationship ruined, or even our very own death, putting God first is totally worth it! Think of John the Baptist who gave his head for following Christ. Think of Paul who was beaten, jailed, and eventually executed for following Christ. Think of all of the past and MODERN missionaries who are martyred for their faith. Would you or I be willing to make such a sacrifice? Naturally, the right answer would be, "Yes, if that is what God asked of me." But, in reality, it seems fair to wonder how many of us would actually just walk away from our faith rather than having to pay a steep cost for obeying and following Christ? I'm afraid, and it's just my humble opinion, that the number of people who would choose health, safety, prosperity, and life will be larger than the ones who accept and gladly pay the price of belonging to Jesus.

To be sure, all costs are not equal. As I was thinking about some of my most memorable ministry experiences, I recalled a hilarious (only in hindsight) story from an evangelism trip to Mozambique, Africa not long ago. The trip was going extremely well. We planned to share the Jesus video there, in the evenings. However, where we were staying was about an hour and a half boat ride from where we were going to show the video. So, the friendly people of that country were going to let us stay in one of their villages that night. Pretty awesome, right?

Well, we showed the video once it got dark enough for the projector, and it was wonderfully successful. Hundreds gave their life to Christ that evening! Afterwards, my team was walking back to where we were going to stay for the night, in the pitch black, with two very small flashlights. The Americans had them, not the people of the village (lol, they knew where *they* were going and they were not afraid of the dark).

We entered this very small straw and mud shack. We walked into a tiny second room of it and there on the floor were two 2-foot by 6-foot foam mats. They said this was where we would be sleeping. I was with my great friend, Jimmy May, who was leading this mission trip and our interpreter, Harry Luhanga.

I stood there and was taking it all in. My little mind was processing where I was about to lay my head down for the night. And then, through the small gleam of the flashlight, I noticed something on the floor. There were ANTS by the GAZILLION. They were everywhere! I told Harry that these ants were going to get up on our mats. He told me that they didn't do that. They stayed only on the floor. I couldn't believe that was true. But this is where we were told to sleep.

Here's where it gets hilariously interesting. There are two mats on the floor with ants crawling all around. By this time, I am halfway freaking out over this situation. I stopped staring at the mats and turned around and there was Jimmy, my team leader, stripped down to his underwear! I said, "Jimmy, what are you doing? These two mats are not big enough for you and me to be laying here with ants on the ground and you in your underwear." He told me he couldn't sleep with all his clothes on. It was starting to feel awkward. I turned back around, and now *Harry* was taking off *his* pants! I said, "Harry what the heck are you doing?" He said that he was sleeping with us! I said, "Harry, there are only two mats and there surely can't be enough room for all three of us." I was feeling even more than awkward at this time. I was lying on a mat in between two guys in their underwear, with ants on the floor. I prayed that God would let the dawn come very quickly.

After a short time of lying there, Harry suddenly sat straight up in our mat bed. Needless to say, this got my attention. He found my flashlight and started shining it on our mat bed. There were ants all over it! Now I really was freaking out. I started to somewhat yell at Harry and tell him, "I told you so! I told you that these ants were going to get on us!" By this time, Jimmy woke up and is wondering what's going on. We turned the flashlight to him and there are ants all over his back and belly. Not only was I sleeping in-between two men in their underwear, but now the ants were crawling all over us.

We jumped up and started brushing ants off of our bodies. Harry went and got another man from the village. He came in and put something on the mats and told us to go back to bed.

Needless to say, I enjoyed very little sleep that night.

It was fabulously funny <u>after</u> the fact. I had never done anything like it before and I am here to tell you that I have never done anything like it again.

But in the bigger picture, because we stayed the night, hundreds of people came to faith in Jesus Christ. What are a few ants on your body, and being stuck between two men in their underwear, compared to people receiving Christ as their Lord and Savior? I would do it again for the same results. But maybe next time I could talk those men into keeping, at least, half of their clothes on!

So, again, not all costs are the same. Sometimes it's only money. Sometimes it might cost you a friend in order to follow Jesus. Sometimes it might just be physically uncomfortable, such as sleeping on the floor, with the bugs. Whatever the costs are for you, take up your cross daily (Luke 9:23) and follow Him no matter where it may lead you. He is our God. He is sovereign. He will take care of us. He will provide for us. Someday, we will live with Him in heaven above without any more costs. We will be home. Praise God for that promise someday! But in the here and now, the hardships that we willingly endure and the personal costs of following Christ are often the surest ways to know who the true disciples are versus the ones who only *say* they are Christians.

**My oldest son praying with a
complete stranger.**

CHAPTER 11

GOD-In-The-Box

MANY OF US grew up with Jack-in-the-box. But most of us, in one way or another, have also put God in a box. True statement? We try to limit God on what He can do. I know it sounds crazy, but that is exactly what we do. You and I think that God can only do what we *allow* Him to do. The truth is that God is God and if He really wants to do something, I can promise you that you and I don't have the power to contain or restrain Him as God.

"Ye of little faith" is what comes to my mind. Our faith can be so small from time to time. But why? Don't we serve the one and only true God? Don't we serve the God who alone can save? Don't we serve the God who created the heavens and the earth and everything within? Then, who are we to try and put limitations on God? Or, put God in a box? Or what about just doubting that God can *really* do all of the things He claims to have the power to do? The truth is that WE are the finites and God is the Infinite.

How many times in my life did I say that it <u>can't</u> be done, or that so and so will <u>never</u> be saved. Was I just playing God? If so, I did a pretty crappy job of it! By the way, none of my "practical" advice in this book means anything whatsoever if you are not completely confident that God can do absolutely anything He desires to do. But once you open your mind and heart to the fact that God is large and in charge, you will get to see him work through and around you in truly amazing ways.

In the Book of James, it talks about the Lord's will being done (James 4:15). That is how we should be looking at this life and everything in it. In the South they say, "Lord willing and if the creek don't rise?" Well I am not sure on the latter part, but the first part certainly teaches us something. Why not pray, "Lord I want to please you and do whatever it is you want me to do. I don't want to do it my way. I want to do it how you have shown me or how you are teaching me?" Wow. What a concept for us to grasp ahold of and to never let go. How can we get that in tune with God? I think of the Lord's prayer:

Our Father which art in heaven, Hallowed be
thy name.
Thy kingdom come, Thy will be done in earth, as it
is in heaven.
Give us this day our daily bread.
And forgive us our debts, as we forgive our debtors.
And lead us not into temptation, but deliver us from
evil: For thine is the kingdom, and the power, and
the glory, for ever. Amen. (Matthew 6:9-13, KJV)

How amazing would it be to stay that in-tune with the
Father? If you pray that and mean it, you are giving
God the Father permission (which He does not need)
for Him to have His way in our lives each day. We
must remember that His name is Holy, not ours. We
are His, not the other way around. This is true every
day, not just the days that we *think* we need Him. We
need Jesus every day of our lives. When you're high on
the mountain top, some people think we don't need
Him because everything is going so well. Do you
know why it's going so well? It's because He has you
and is watching over your every step. Some folks think
they don't need Jesus when its going well, but it's going well because of His grace.

Then there are those who only call on His name,
when they are down in the valley. My fellow readers,

God is the same whether you are on the mountain top or down in the valley. He does not change. That is why we need Christ <u>daily</u>. Plead to have that daily bread with Him. Why would anybody want to try and do this life without Him? They shouldn't and to be honest, they truly can't. Pay attention and really try and see if you are ignoring God slightly more when things seem to be going well. And, try and catch yourself if you are mainly only calling out to Him when you are in a valley of some sort. God deserves to have us long to have Him in our lives 24/7/365, regardless of present circumstances.

The Lord's Prayer also talks about forgiving others. This is worthy of discussion because it's related to striving to be like Christ and serving him 24/7 and not just when it is convenient. Why shouldn't we forgive others? Did Christ Himself forgive you and me? He has set the bar high for us to follow Him. Is it easy? Not usually. But is it worth it? Yes, for sure. Matthew West, a Christian contemporary artist, has a song called *Forgiveness*. One of the lyrics stanzas says this:

So, let it go and be amazed by what you see through eyes of grace. The prisoner that it really frees is you. Forgiveness, forgiveness, forgiveness, forgiveness.

If for no other reason, forgive so it can free you from the burden of the grudge or the unforgiveness. You have heard people many times in your life say, I am so glad I got rid of that burden. I have given it to God. I have forgiven so and so and I feel so much better. The Lord is so good at releasing you from the burdens that you and I put upon ourselves from time to time. This matters, because reaching people for Christ isn't just about *doing* or *saying* the right things. We have to *be* the person God wants us to be in order to *do* the things that God wants us to do.

Finally, when I see the end of the Lord's prayer, I come to terms that this is truly God's kingdom, not mine. If I haven't mentioned it before now, know that this is the Lord's show. If we want to follow Him, we have to learn to play by His rules. He did not ask you or me for advice way back when, so with that in mind, let us learn to follow His lead, His guidance, His direction and His way.

For you horse people reading this book, let me share an illustration of how horses and people can be in-tune with one another; and if people and horses can be in perfect harmony, then surely people and God can be in-tune with one another. Look at a cutting horse and its rider. When the rider walks his horse into the arena, he cuts one cow out of the herd. Once the cow is singled out, the rider drops his hand, meaning he puts his hand down upon the withers and cannot move his hand more than an inch in any way. The horse then instinctively (or by the training process) proceeds to keep the cow cut out of the herd, meaning that it won't let the cow get back with its buddies. The horse and rider then continue on for 2 ½ minutes on two or three different cows. They are so in-tune with one another, that the horse needs no reining. He simply knows what to do. The rider can use his feet, but for the most part, the horse does the cutting on its own.

I have used this as a sermon illustration many times. The horse and rider gliding across the arena knowing each other and understanding each other. What if you and I could have that kind of relationship with our Lord and Savior? I want to be so in tuned with Christ while He leads me that it looks even better than a well-trained cutting horse.

For those of you who know me, you might have heard me say that I also want to be so full of the Holy Spirit, that when a mosquito bites me, I want him to be flying away singing, *there's power in the blood, there's power in the blood.* Funny, right? But those are the two main ingredients for being best equipped to serve God: Submitted to His will and way of doing things, and empowered by the Holy Spirit. This is how we can

get (and remain) in-tune with Christ and begin impact-
ing the lives of those around us.

When I allow myself to drift away from Christ, even
a little, that's when my life starts to take a downhill
turn. That is bad for me (obviously), and bad for my
family, but it is also bad news for everyone on earth
that God has planned for me to be a witness to. But
when I am walking with the Lord daily, as He desires,
and praying constantly for the filling of the Holy Spirit,
and setting my mind to accomplishing God's plans for
the day rather than my own, then I find balance in life
and experience the true joy of belonging to and serving God.

Staying with the idea of being in-tune, let me address
our relationships with our spouses. It is pretty tough to
be on the same page with your spouse when you are
not on the same page; in fact, it typically doesn't work
out. So, how does a man and a woman learn to get on
the same page? Well that is a great question. I can only
tell you how Rebecca and I did it and offer a couple of
examples.

I would like for everybody to know that my wife is
as pretty as they come. We have been married over 26
years. She is a beautiful woman both inside and out.
Once you meet her, you will understand what I am
talking about. She loves the Lord with every ounce in

her body. Over the years she has learned to become a wonderful preacher's wife, also. Did you catch the key word there? *Learned.* When God called me to the ministry, I explained to my wife what I felt the Lord was telling me to do. In the very beginning, she was great with it. But within a couple of years, with all the changes going on to our lives, she began to have second thoughts. We butted heads a few times and things were a little rough. One night we had both finally had enough of the bickering, and she said these devastating words to me: "You might have been called to the ministry, but I wasn't." Whoa. That sure took the air out of my sails. But she meant it and I'm glad she said it out loud. Because, that day changed our relationship and ministry life, thank God, forever for the better!

I had come to realize (with Rebecca's help!) that I was leaving my wife out on so many decisions and ideas that God was giving to me. Instead of her helping me, she was running after me trying to catch up to me. I was doing ministry without her and doing it selfishly. I had a decision to make. Either, I could continue to chase God on my own, and watch my marriage get weaker and weaker. Or, I could swallow my pride, repent of my sin, and beg my wife for the opportunity to try harder and do a much better job of including her in the picture. Thankfully, she agreed and we, essentially, hit the reset button on our ministry.

She had some great, godly girlfriends who helped her along the way. I also had a mentor, Mark Dickson, my best friend in South Dakota, who was trying his best to slow me down a little and get me more strongly rooted in some important aspects of ministry. To say the least, Rebecca and I were not on the same page in the beginning, but oh boy are we there today! We both praise God for what He has done on that front. Guys typically get an idea and we just run with it. That's not always a bad thing, but men, if you are married, your wife is an equal partner in whatever you do. Not only that, but she has a God-given mission to help and support you in fulfilling the ministry to which God has called you BOTH. Trust me, wives take that role very seriously and they do not intend to fail, because they know their call is from God. It is no wonder why wives get a little agitated when they feel left out in the ministry.

I love looking into Ephesians chapter 5. Verse 22 says, "Wives, submit yourselves unto your own husbands, as unto the Lord" (KJV). Verse 23 then says, "For the husband is the head of the wife, even as Christ is the head of the church: and he is the savior of the body" (KJV). Verse 24 then reads, "Therefore as the church is subject unto Christ, so let the wives be to their own husbands in every thing" (KJV). Here are three powerful verses that provide enormous guidance for our wives. Yet, if you are a man, at some point in the past you have likely misinterpreted this passage. I know I sure did and had to learn things the hard way.

I will never forget after Rebecca and I became Christians, I was reading the Bible one day. I thought I had found the holy grail (for dudes). I read verse 22 and boy was I excited. I ran to my wife and tried to tell her that I could now prove that I had been right for all of these years. I said, "I told you, babe, that I was supposed to be the boss and you are supposed to listen to me." Then I showed her that verse. I believe it was about a week later, maybe more, when she finally spoke to me the next time (lol). There I was trying to show what the Good Book said, but I was getting punished for it. What? I couldn't understand what I had done wrong. Boy did I sure have a lot to learn back then.

When my wife finally spoke to me, she asked me if I had read any more? I said "No, I was just shocked when I learned what <u>you</u> were supposed to be doing <u>for me</u>." She said very calmly, "Go read the rest of that chapter." So, I did and here was the *real* holy grail:

> ²⁵ Husbands, love your wives, even as Christ also loved the church, and gave himself for it;

²⁶ That he might sanctify and cleanse it with the washing of water by the word,

²⁷ That he might present it to himself a glorious church, not having spot, or wrinkle, or any such thing; but that it should be holy and without blemish.

²⁸ So ought men to love their wives as their own bodies. He that loveth his wife loveth himself.

²⁹ For no man ever yet hated his own flesh; but nourisheth and cherisheth it, even as the Lord the church:

³⁰ For we are members of his body, of his flesh, and of his bones.

³¹ For this cause shall a man leave his father and mother, and shall be joined unto his wife, and they two shall be one flesh.

³² This is a great mystery: but I speak concerning Christ and the church.

³³ Nevertheless let every one of you in particular so love his wife even as himself; and the wife see that she reverence her husband. (Ephesians 5:25-33 KJV)

Whoa. I had no idea. The women have three verses and we men have an entire paragraph! Again, having not learned anything from my previous mistake, I got myself into trouble right away. Rebecca asked me what I thought. My first thought was, why on earth did Paul continue to write? Maybe he should have just stopped at verse 24. Then I looked at my wife and (finally!) started to figure out what she was trying to tell me. Being the typical man, I had missed the point. Yes, most women will submit to the man as the head of the household, but men, we don't need to remind them of this. I also learned that it is much better for a woman to read Ephesians 5:22 on her own and understand it than have a (um, slow-to-learn) husband like myself read it and point it out to her.

It is also true that in Genesis chapter 2, the Bible calls the woman a man's *helpmate* or *helper*. It makes no mention that the woman is to be a slave to the husband, or be ordered around by the husband. It simply implies that God's work is important, and so the husband and wife will have to strive together to get it done. These are things that I have learned over the years. This is why my wife and I now have a much stronger relationship. Today my wife and I can joke about some of these things. But most assuredly, I can tell you that when those early disagreements were actually happening, there was no joking going on. My wife wanted to help me and wanted me to succeed, but I was trying to do ministry without her. It was hurtful and frustrating to her, and It was a huge mistake that I was making. I would urge every reader to make sure you serve God with your spouse completely on board.

Today, it is so much different and better. We discuss matters intelligently with one another, we make our plans together, and we pray together which is the most important thing. When a man and a woman come together to pray to the One who created them, it is just plain powerful. In fact, something that most people do not know about us is that whenever we pray, whether at home, in a church, or anywhere else, whenever possible we always hold each other's hands. Why? Not to be too literal, but when we pray, we truly want to be in <u>one</u> accord. My prayer is her prayer and vice versa. There is power when two become one and both are sold out to Christ.

Men, let me ask you, when was the last time you held your wife's hand? If it has been awhile, then I encourage you to do this very thing tonight. When was the last time you held your wife's hand and prayed together? That's probably been even longer, right? Like I said, I wasn't doing a good job of this either. But honestly, how do we ever expect to get in tune with one another, if we can't even pray with one another? Men if you want your wife to humbly submit to you, then you had better learn to treat her like a princess. Be soft and gentle with them. They are not a sack of feed to be tossed around. They are like a flower (not weak, but in need of attention and care). Water them and nurture them and they will bloom. Neglect them or stomp on them, and they will simply wilt and go away. It is your choice. I choose the first one, because I have tried the second one and I never want that experience again. I thank God that He has saved my marriage more than once.

I am not trying to make this part of the book about Rebecca or me, because the truth is that it is all about Christ. But because it is all about Christ, it means serving Him as a <u>team</u> is a double-blessing for us, but is also glorifying to God. Husbands and wives must learn to minister alongside one another. Wives will usually have different roles than husbands. Both have to do what they have been called by God and gifted to do. The husband's work is not more important than the wife's, and neither is her work more important than his. When the two become one, though, it is definitely a force. And this is what we need more of among Christians if we are to have the kind of impact on the world that God expects us to have.

I am just so thankful that God has given my wife a LOT of patience, and that I have been able to come around (slowly at times) to be a better husband for her.

She deserves it. She has put up with me for all these years. There is no one else I would rather do this life with than Rebecca Scott. She has encouraged me one hundred-fold more than I will probably ever be able to encourage her. I am getting better, but men let us never take for granted how important our wives are to us.

Women, please don't ever give up on your men. If you think we are hopeless now, trust me, it could be worse. If we seem hopeless with you IN our lives, just imagine how ugly it would be with you OUT of our lives. I don't know what some of you ladies might be working with in terms of a husband. But I sure do encourage you to hang in there, because believe it or not, the majority of men do get a few things figured out at some point in their lives.

I imagine that most women already pray for their husbands. If you are not a praying wife, or you honestly know that you could do better, I hope you will consider some of the things in this section of the book. We have some friends whom we have known for years, Kraig and Michelle Emmett. Kraig and I should have gone to jail together back in the day, but the Lord spared that as well (lol…long story that'll have to go in a different book). After God saved me and called me into the ministry, He laid on my heart to do a men's event which I named CatchAFIRE. My friend, Kraig, came to the very first one. I watched as the speaker gave an invitation and my friend went forward. Kraig got saved at the first men's CatchAFIRE held back in 2013. It was awesome. I hugged him so tightly that night and told him how proud of him I was. It changed his life, dramatically.

Here is where the prayer comes in. We were over at Kraig and Michelle's house having supper one night. Michelle asked me if I would pray for the meal. I was within about a second of saying, "let's pray." At that moment, Kraig choked up a little and then said, "guys let's pray for our meal." I looked over at Michelle and she had tears running down her cheeks. She had been praying for her husband for many years and then right in front of her eyes, her husband was beginning to come around. This was over eight years ago. We still talk about it from time to time. God can change anybody's heart. If Michelle can pray and see her husband come to faith in Christ, and then see him begin to exercise spiritual leadership in the home, then the readers of this book can do it too. How might you need to begin praying for *your* spouse? Look, prayer works! It isn't because we offer special prayers at specific times, with our eyes closed just right. Prayer works because of the One who hears and responds to the prayers. It is the way, through Christ, that we stay connected with our Heavenly Father and speak with Him daily.

One more quick story to show how faithful and praying wives can have an impact on unbelieving husbands. Rebecca and I know a couple who are in their 70's. The wife has been saved for many years. I saw her one day in town and asked about her husband who I knew wasn't a believer. She told me that her husband had been saved at church a few months ago. She said his cussing had almost all but stopped (Yes, I know that doesn't prove someone is saved, but in this case, he truly was transformed by faith in Christ). She told me that he now loves to go to church because he is learning and actually "gets" spiritual things now. As is the case so much of the time, he had "attended" church with her for years, but he only did so because she wanted him to. She went on to tell me that now they always pray together for their meals. I asked her how long she had prayed for her husband to be saved? She said **"I prayed for him for over 40 years."**

My friends, 40 years is a very long time. But 40 years is not nearly as long as is an eternity without Christ. Spouses, please hear my heart on this: DON'T EVER GIVE UP PRAYING FOR THEM. In reality, it is very likely that everybody but *you* have already given up on them, so you might be their last hope for salvation. Forty years of praying and her prayers were finally answered. Keep this story in your mind when praying for your spouse. God does not always answer prayers in one day, or one week, or one month, or even one year. But rest assured, He is listening and He is sovereign. When God, in His infinite wisdom, determines to act on your prayers, it is going to be mind-blowing.

You, my friend, must be faithful and continue to do your part (witnessing) and God will do His part (saving). Today I am thankful for praying wives who never cease praying for their husbands. I believe there is a tremendous blessing in store for those faithful ones. I spoke with the husband, and congratulated him on his being born again. I asked him why it took so long. He said, "It just did. I regret not getting saved earlier. Now I only have a small amount of time left to glorify our God."

It is pretty powerful to think about it like that. I have always personally said something similar. I didn't get saved until I was 27. I wished I had been saved in junior high school. If I had been, I would have done a lot of things differently back in the day. But the bottom line is that nobody can be saved until God the Father draws that person to Himself (John 6:44). I wasn't ready to be saved until I was 27. I don't know why. But when it was my time, I knew it and I was ready. That couple above is now more in tune with each other because of their common denominator – God. She was faithful to pray daily for her husband and God was more than faithful to cause this man to be saved.

Ms. Jane being baptized
at 87 years old (it's never
too late as long as you're
still alive)

CHAPTER 12

Coronaviris Pandemic but Still Serving the Lord

THE EPIC PANDEMIC

Something pretty crazy happened in the world between the time I finished my original manuscript for this book and the time it was to go to the publisher. A global virus pandemic swept the world and may have changed American society forever. Since no disease on earth can touch the Word of God or change the Gospel message, I did not originally intend to even include anything about Covid-19 in this book. However, it has dramatically affected daily life for billions of people around the world. Churches were ordered closed by the government. Social distancing and mask-wearing rules made ministry more challenging. So, I decided to include this short chapter.

This pandemic wreaked havoc all across the globe. It

was a virus that was originally found in Wuhan, China in December, 2019. It was called Covid-19, also known as the Coronavirus. The virus was a respiratory disease. The symptoms were much like the common flu bug: fever, cough and shortness of breath. The shortness of breath is what caused a lot of panic, which then led to large numbers of hospitalizations and additional panic. Other symptoms of the virus included: fatigue, muscle pain, diarrhea, sore throat, loss of smell, and abdominal pain. As you can see, without an actual test, if you contracted this virus you might have thought it was just the flu bug or you might have thought you were sure to die. The whole thing was quite the challenge (and still is even as I'm writing this). While most people did recover, there were many deaths associated with this virus as well. As of the middle of August 2020, more than 21 million cases had been reported worldwide resulting in over 761,000 deaths.

Those are big numbers, but in a world of 8 billion people, what was the big deal? People die every day, right? They sure do, which is one of the reasons I wrote this book. We have to get the Gospel to folks because time is short for so many. But it wasn't just the deaths. How this virus came out of nowhere just seemed to make the whole world go crazy. People went absolutely bonkers with fear and the people of the United

States were no different. One of the first things that we saw even in little bitty rural towns in Wyoming was that people started buying up all of the toilet paper. Yes, that is correct. Toilet paper went off the shelves like mad. Also, all cleaning supplies, including: Lysol, disinfectant wipes, hand sanitizer and about all other paper products were gone in a flash. For a month or so, sugar, flour, bread, milk, eggs, potatoes, canned goods and even some meat products were in very short supply. The grocery stores put limits on most items. People were panic-buying and hoarders were out doing what hoarders do best - hoarding. Small town living was much better than living in a large city at the time (I have to imagine). But this whole ordeal was/is quite stressful.

For a while, masks and latex gloves were being used by over half of the population. The virus tended to claim the lives of the older generations and those who had underlying medical conditions. The coronavirus had affected the entire world in just a few months. It shut down things that most people would not believe possible: bars, restaurants, casinos, most small businesses, and virtually all non-essential services, just shut down. Every school in the country was forced to close its doors by the middle of March. It gets worse. Every church in our country was kindly asked to shut its doors until after the threat of this virus had subsided. The stock markets crashed, losing nearly 30% of its monies. Our crude oil was being traded on the stock market for a *negative* sum. It was like nothing anybody alive had ever gone through before.

Aside from churches being temporarily closed, here is where things really began to affect ministry and evangelism. We had this thing called social distancing. It was a mandate from the health officials of the United States to stay at least six feet apart from other people. They asked that people not shake hands or hug. No gatherings of more than 10 people at any given place. There was no visitation allowed in hospitals or nursing homes. Parents and grand-parents were passing away in those facilities, and nobody from the outside world was allowed to be in there with them. Funerals were put on hold until it was "safe" to be in contact with people once again. It was a sad time in our America.

By the time this book was being sent to the publisher, things were starting to look a little better for our great country. Individual states were opening back up and started to let the private sector go back to work. Schools had all been canceled for the remaining school year, with great hopes that they would reopen in the fall as scheduled, which seems to be happening in more cases than not.

The reason I have included this information about the virus in this book, is to share with folks what ministry looked like during the time of this pandemic. Because, guess what? This wasn't the worst thing that has ever happened in the history of the world. And even if it was, God is still on His throne and still expects the work to get done. I was *still* a preacher. A preacher must share the Good News with people. For a travelling preacher, like myself, it got quite difficult. About the middle of March, 2020, I was outside of Nashville, Tennessee when things really started to go awry. All of the churches that I was scheduled to preach in were calling and cancelling. A revival that had been scheduled for several months in Texas was cancelled as well. I'll never forget flying back home on a Boeing 737 aircraft with about 25 people on board. It was the smallest number of folks I had ever seen on a plane of that size. The bright side of that was that we could sit wherever we wanted. Hey, you have to claim even the small victories!

Churches were not "allowed" to have corporate worship as usual. Many churches in the country went to drive-in worship service formats. Also, most churches had some form of on-line preaching or teaching every Sunday. A lot of pastors, like me, started preaching on Facebook live. Personally, I chose Friday nights to do my on-line Facebook live sermons. I had preached at a cowboy church in Georgia on Friday nights before. I asked the pastor there why he chose to preach on Friday nights. He said it was because the man before him who started the church was a drunk. When he got saved, and was clean and sober, he told God that if He could use a former drunk to lead people to Him, then he would start to preach on Friday nights. He knew what he did back in the day on Friday nights, so he wanted to offer to others an option to worship Jesus instead of going to the bars. I came to really enjoy that story. So, when I prayed and asked God for guidance on when to do a weekly sermon, it became quite obvious to me.

A message that I had been telling the church for years was now playing out in front of our eyes. The church needs to learn to be the church outside of the four walls of the church. When the physical church buildings were locked on Sundays, yes, it looked like a very negative and sad development. But in reality, it presented the perfect opportunity for growth for many Christians. I had been telling the church that it needs to get busy *outside* of the physical building. Now, there wasn't even a choice about it. The church had left the building! I'm not saying that closing down churches was a good thing. But I *am* saying that doing the Lord's work outside of Sunday mornings was long overdue and many good things have already come of it. For example, I now preach *online* every single Friday night. That is a message that wasn't happening before and reaches an audience that wasn't being reached before. In fact, I happen to know that some of the folks who tune in to my Friday messages are very unlikely (at least at this point in their lives) to walk into a traditional, physical Sunday morning church service. I am blessed that God uses me in this fashion to meet people right where they are, right in their living rooms and kitchens, DURING a global virus pandemic. God is good!

I have received countless messages and phone calls from people stating that they were glad that we were doing church on-line. People were actually listening AND responding to the preaching of God's Word. I know in my heart that people were being saved because they were hearing the Gospel of Jesus Christ. Yes, people get saved even outside of the church and even on days other than Sundays. The Gospel was penetrating souls during this time that might not have ever heard the Good News if the church hadn't been "shut down" for a short time. God was using something (virus pandemic and church shutdowns) that most people had concluded was unbelievably bad, and contrary to conventional wisdom, used it to bring glory to Himself.

Prayer chains were everywhere during this time. People prayed over the phones, through Zoom (an Internet meeting place) and over all types of online social media. My good friend, Kate Hunter, from Whitewood, South Dakota put together a 24-hour prayer vigil. So, on a particular Saturday night at 12:00 am, people from all across the country took one hour over the next 24 hours and prayed fervently for our nation and the people. I cannot begin to count how many times I saw the command given to Solomon in 2 Chronicles 7:14 shared or stated: "if my people who are called by my name, will humble themselves and pray and seek my face and turn from their wicked ways, then I will hear from heaven, and I will forgive their sin and will heal their land" (NIV). People "prayed" this over and over.

I found it quite interesting that so many people seem to believed that 2 Chronicles 7:14 is a prayer. It's not really a prayer at all but a command given to Solomon after he had finished building the temple. Now, an *actual* prayer that I thought I should have seen more is found in the book of Daniel:

> [3] Then I set my face toward the Lord God to make request by prayer and supplications, with fasting, sackcloth, and ashes. [4] And I prayed to the Lord

my God, and made confession, and said, "O Lord, great and awesome God, who keeps His covenant and mercy with those who love Him, and with those who keep His commandments, [5] we have sinned and committed iniquity, we have done wickedly and rebelled, even by departing from Your precepts and Your judgments. [6] Neither have we heeded Your servants the prophets, who spoke in Your name to our kings and our princes, to our fathers and all the people of the land. [7] O Lord, righteousness *belongs* to You, but to us shame of face, as *it is* this day—to the men of Judah, to the inhabitants of Jerusalem and all Israel, those near and those far off in all the countries to which You have driven them, because of the unfaithfulness which they have committed against You.

[8] "O Lord, to us *belongs* shame of face, to our kings, our princes, and our fathers, because we have sinned against You. [9] To the Lord our God *belong* mercy and forgiveness, though we have rebelled against Him. [10] We have not obeyed the voice of the Lord our God, to walk in His laws, which He set before us by His servants the prophets. [11] Yes, all Israel has transgressed Your law, and has departed so as not to obey Your voice; therefore the curse and the oath written

in the Law of Moses the servant of God have been poured out on us, because we have sinned against Him. ¹² And He has confirmed His words, which He spoke against us and against our judges who judged us, by bringing upon us a great disaster; for under the whole heaven such has never been done as what has been done to Jerusalem.

¹³ "As *it is* written in the Law of Moses, all this disaster has come upon us; yet we have not made our prayer before the Lord our God, that we might turn from our iniquities and understand Your truth. ¹⁴ Therefore the Lord has kept the disaster in mind, and brought it upon us; for the Lord our God *is* righteous in all the works which He does, though we have not obeyed His voice. ¹⁵ And now, O Lord our God, who brought Your people out of the land of Egypt with a mighty hand, and made Yourself a name, as *it is* this day—we have sinned, we have done wickedly! ¹⁶ "O Lord, according to all Your righteousness, I pray, let Your anger and Your fury be turned away from Your city Jerusalem, Your holy mountain; because for our sins, and for the iniquities of our fathers, Jerusalem and Your people *are* a reproach to all *those* around us. ¹⁷ Now therefore, our God,

hear the prayer of Your servant, and his supplications, and for the Lord's sake cause Your face
to shine on Your sanctuary, which is desolate. [18]
O my God, incline Your ear and hear; open Your
eyes and see our desolations, and the city which
is called by Your name; for we do not present our
supplications before You because of our righteous
deeds, but because of Your great mercies. [19] O
Lord, hear! O Lord, forgive! O Lord, listen and
act! Do not delay for Your own sake, my God,
for Your city and Your people are called by Your
name. (Daniel 9:3-19, NKJV).

I believe this was a prayer that should have been
prayed more in 2020. In my humble opinion, this is
one of the very best prayers in all of the Bible. Daniel
prayed and confessed. That is what we should have
been doing all along, not only praying but also confessing our sin to God above. Most people wanted
God to *fix* our virus problem, when in reality, God was
more interested in people confessing their sins and
turning from their wicked ways. He wanted people to
repent and come back to Him. Yes, some did do that,
but others stayed their courses and kept on with their
same lifestyle and belief system. Maybe this virus was
another avenue God was using to get our attention. If it

was, He surely had *my* attention. From the onset of this virus, my wife and I prayed every single day for God's hand to be shown and for His will to be done. I won't be able to tell you in this book how long we prayed for this situation (because it is ongoing at the moment), but rest assured we will pray for this situation until it is resolved.

My whole point with all of this is that ministry did <u>not</u> cease during this time. We just had to find other ways to reach people with the Gospel. I remember seeing on social media one day, a meme that read, "and all of a sudden all pastors were now televangelists." It was sort of true. Preachers have to preach and they do need a congregation of some type. Although we could not have a live audience, we still preached the Gospel to a camera of some sort in hopes that others would receive the fuel they needed to continue to get through this pandemic.

Here is another example of how even a global pandemic can't stop God's work, and why we must always be ready to step up and serve when the Spirit is moving. At the time of this writing, I had preached at the retirement center in Basin, Wyoming for nearly nine years. During the Covid-19 crisis, they had not let me in to preach to my "elder folks." In July, 2020, after not being able to minister to these wonderful seniors at all for a few months, we at least started to meet and preach via Zoom. It was better than nothing.

About six weeks into our Zoom experience, I preached one Thursday about Phillip and the Ethiopian Eunuch. After the sermon, I asked if any of the residents had anything they wanted to say. One of the ladies said, "Pastor James, I have something to say." So, I told Ms. Jane, "Go ahead, you have the floor." She said that when she was 5 years old, her parents had her christened. She went on to say that she didn't actually get saved until she was 10. Then she said this: "Pastor, I want you to baptize me." All I could say was, "Wow!" This woman was 87. She had been saved for 77 years and had never followed up her profession of faith with baptism. I am obviously not saying that she wasn't truly saved, just because she wasn't baptized. But baptism is mighty important, and it was obviously important to her, which then made it important to me!

After some more conversation, I explained to her that it was going to be no small feat to baptize her during a virus pandemic, especially with her facility locked down tighter than a drum. But I pledged to her that I would do everything I could possibly do to make it happen, but that we would still have to trust the Lord to work out some details. I want you to know that God did some amazing things, through some amazing folks, to be able to help this 87-year-young lady be baptized.

The activities director at Wyoming Retirement Center, Dawn Wehrman, was able to get a platform put in place and a stock tank filled with water. This made it possible for Ms. Jane to be raised up in the "lift" and easily placed into the stock tank. The residents and staff that came out to watch her baptism all had to wear masks and stay 6 feet apart. They asked me to wear a mask and wear latex gloves. It was quite the sight to see! But when it was all over, after 77 years in the making, this beautiful Christian woman was baptized. She was finally able to tell the world, through her baptism, that she had been and was going to follow Jesus Christ for the remainder of her life.

I hope you are uplifted by these stories. Because, even during a pandemic like we were going through, God was still on the throne. He was still working through His people to advance the Kingdom of Christ. It is a lesson for believers to not run and hide just because our earthly circumstances get tougher. It is during times like these, very often, that God chooses to do some of His mightiest work. Some Christians will choose to lay low when times are challenging, but you and I need to say to God, "Here am I, send me" (Isaiah 6:8, NIV).

Also, since one of the purposes of this book is to help equip all Christians everywhere to do God's work in the world, I want to encourage you to NEVER allow negative circumstances to prevent you from serving the Lord the way He desires. If churches close, go find people to minister to in person. If social distancing doesn't allow you to get close to anybody, then reach them online. If they don't have the Internet, send them an encouraging note through the mail. God's work must go forward. He will give us the wisdom and strength to do whatever needs to be done, so long as we are not retreating from the battle!

One thing that I would say about believers retreating, is that a few too many professing Christians were letting their *fears* be bigger than their *faith*. Where was their faith during this time? Did God somehow just go away? Was God only important when their lives were smooth and simple? What about when people's lives were in the valley? Is God not the God of both the mountain top AND the valley? Did any of this catch God by surprise? A lot of Christians, who passionately believe in the promises of God about eternal life in heaven, were all of a sudden afraid to die. Why? If that would happen to be you, what are you afraid of? To my knowledge, every one of us is going to die someday unless the rapture comes first.

I told a man during this time that whether it was a horse accident, a car wreck, a heart attack or Covid-19 that killed me, it simply did not matter. I was absolutely assured in my faith where I would spend eternity. I'm not bragging about my faith (because it is God's work in me), but that is what absolute faith looks like in Jesus Christ. I am simply not afraid to die. Don't get me wrong, I don't usually wake up every morning and *hope* that it will be my last day. Instead, I wake up every morning and thank the Lord for another day, but if it turned out to be my last day on this earth, that would be fine too. I am totally comfortable with going on to heaven to be with my Lord and Savior. That is what bold confidence in Jesus can do for your personal morale, AND non-Christians need to see our faith too. They don't just need to see our faith when it comes to going to church, taking communion, or studying the Bible. They need to see that our faith is rooted in something that is actually leading us somewhere permanent. Death is not something we are supposed to fear. It is simply a stepping stone to get us to our eternal, heavenly home.

So, without a doubt, life has been different these first few months of 2020. Some folks battled the storm well while others barely stayed afloat. The real-deal Christians never took their eyes off of their Savior during the pandemic. I imagine that many folks were wondering how those Christians were so calm through it all. It's not that we didn't go through the same storm as everybody else, but when you have an eternal perspective, because you are the child of an eternal God, then all of the blips on the road of life just aren't all that scary anymore. When Christ is at the helm of your life, my friend, you can withstand anything that this life throws at you. Why? Because my Jesus told us that He would never leave us nor forsake us. Is the hope that you have as good as the hope that I have? Let's all start truly hoping in Christ together.

Turn the page and let's start the last and in my opinion, the very best advice and truth that I can share with any one person. This last chapter is what drives me to be the person that God has called me to be every single day of my life. Let's get into the details of the Gospel of Jesus Christ!!

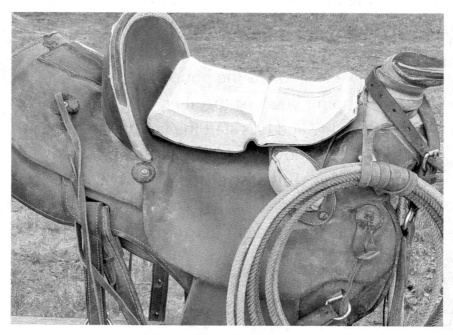

My saddle and my bible. Always ready
at a moments notice to go and share the Word of God

Conclusion: The Gospel of the Lord Jesus Christ

I HAVE TRIED my very best to save the very best for last. Not that the Gospel of Jesus Christ should be last, because it should be first, but I hope that you have learned things and been encouraged and challenged up until this last chapter. I have had many laughs along the way while writing this book. My friends will be glad when I am done. My wife will be relieved when it finally goes to print. Friends, family, church congregations, and probably even a few strangers along the way, have all heard me say at various times, "Funny you should bring that up; I have addressed that in my book!" (lol).

Rebecca will probably be the happiest of anyone that this book is finally coming to a conclusion. Because, the entire time I have been writing, I would look up at her and say, "I'm up to 5,000 words baby; now 10,000 words, 20,000 words," and so on. It has made for great table conversation for many months. I have kept a notebook on my phone of topics to discuss and stories to tell. It has been very meaningful to me to finally have the opportunity to write some of these things down. The stories that I have shared are all so very true. I have not embellished a single thing throughout. With the Lord's help, I have tried to be accurate and to be sensitive to some of the topics. I have used several different translations to quote the Bible verses. I believe this book has numerous *how-to* tips and maybe even a few *what-to-dos* and *what-not-to-dos* as well.

My best friends have encouraged me so much and I am thankful for that. I can't tell you what it's like to have grown men who love me and have taken time out of their lives to help invest in my life. But truly, this is still just a book. The book itself has no saving effect on anybody. When God laid it on my heart to write a book, I already knew what the last chapter would be. I wanted the last to be the very best. So, this last chapter will be totally devoted to the Gospel of Jesus Christ. And that DOES have a saving effect on people.

My prayer is that I have honored Him and brought glory to His name throughout this process. Right before I finished writing, I spoke at a church in Georgia. It was just minutes before I was about to preach and this young man came up to me and asked me if I was nervous. I said "nervous for what?" I looked him square in the eye and boldly said "in a few minutes I get to get up there and tell almost 300 people about my Jesus. Why would I be nervous about that?" I think he got my message loud and clear. We have nothing to be embarrassed, shy, timid, or nervous about when we get the opportunity to tell the world about Jesus. Truly, it is an honor and privilege to tell the world about His goodness and the fact that He is the only way to heaven. So, with all of that said, this will be my very best and intentional effort in sharing the Gospel with you. If you need to respond to the Gospel and put your faith and trust in Christ, then I invite you to do so. If you have already done that, then pass it on.

Romans 3:23 says, "for all have sinned and fall short of the glory of God" (NKJV). That three-letter word, *all*, pretty much signifies every single last person on earth (past, present, and future). We have no choice in the matter. We are sinners. I like to tell people that even their grandma is and was a sinner. We somehow think grandmas are perfect and way too sweet to sin. Maybe in our eyes it's true, but in the eyes of the Lord, they are still sinners who need a Savior.

Romans 5:8 says, "But God demonstrates His own love toward us, in that while we were still sinners,

Christ died for us" (NKJV). Even when I didn't know God and even when I ran *from* God, He had already sent His son, Jesus Christ, to die on the cross for me. Heck, there was a time in my life when I didn't even believe that there was a God. But you guessed it, God had already sent Jesus to the cross to die for me (and you). His love for us is immeasurable and truly unconditional.

My favorite verse of the Romans Road is Romans 6:23, "for the wages of sin is death, but the gift of God is eternal life in Christ Jesus our Lord" (NKJV). Jesus's death on the cross was an absolutely free gift to you and to me and to all who would receive it. It did not cost you or I anything for Christ to die on that cross. But I ask you this: How much did it cost God? It cost God His one and only Son. Christ's death on the cross is and was an absolutely free gift to each person who would repent and receive. The sacrifice by the Father, through the Son, demonstrates the depths of God's love for us. I certainly urge sinners to give this serious thought before even thinking of rejecting this wonderful gift.

Parents, think about it like this: God willingly did what no parent on the face of this earth could ever do. From our earthly perspective, He had to do something that was unthinkable and unimaginable. Yet, God went through with the sacrifice, and He did it for you and me. The gift is completely available, free, and there for the taking. But many people never accept it. Matthew 7:13-14 are very clear in this matter: "Enter by the narrow gate; for wide is the gate and broad is the way that leads to destruction, and there are many who go in by it. Because narrow is the gate and difficult is the way which leads to life, and there are few who find it" (NKJV). I think about all the people who have heard the message but never believed it to be truth. They are on that road that leads to hell. In fact, many (actually most) people are on that road, and it breaks my heart. I was on that road for 27 years of my life. I never want to go back to that road ever again.

I have heard the Gospel, I have believed it to be true, I have repented of my sins, and someday I will spend my eternity in Heaven above with Jesus Christ. It won't be because I tried really hard to *live* the right way, but rather it will be because Jesus Christ lives within me. But verse 14 should scare the daylights out of us. Enter through the narrow way, which is a way that only a few will find.

How do you distinguish between broad and narrow? Broad is like a six-lane Interstate with cars flying up and down the lanes at 80 miles per hour. I doubt that is exactly the image Matthew had in mind 2,000 years ago, but that is what I imagine "broad" looking like. If you are from the country, you may know what a two-track looks like. A two-track is a dirt road with, literally, just enough room for one vehicle to drive down and usually has grass or weeds growing up in the middle of it. You can obviously tell that there is not much traffic on a road like this. That, in my mind, is what the narrow and lesser traveled road looks like.

Now, in light of Matthew 7:13-14, which road are you on and which road do you want to be on? Your choice is broad, easy, and popular (but it leads to destruction) versus narrow, difficult, and fairly deserted (yet it leads to eternal life). Would it help if I told you I have been on both roads in my lifetime? But I don't ever want to go back to the broad road. It was nothing but hustle, bustle and sin. That path was so wide, I was able to do my own thing my own way, and rarely thought twice about God. I am grateful that God has set me on the narrow path.

It is a flat-out wonderful journey to be going down that narrow road with the Lord. So, no matter where you currently are, just know that God has made it possible for you to switch directions in life. He has given us the gift of His Son, Jesus Christ. If you are willing to reach out and accept that gift, accept Christ into your life, then you will instantly be on the path that leads to eternity in Heaven. It's right in front of you, right now. It is your move my friend. Will you accept the gift of eternal life that God is offering, or will you reject it like so many that have come before? It is up to you!

Romans 10:9-10 says, "that if you confess with your mouth the Lord Jesus and believe in your heart that God has raised Him from the dead, you will be saved. For with the heart one believes unto righteousness, and with the mouth confession is made unto salvation" (NKJV). This is kind of a two-part process. I have known people my whole life that know who God is but have never made a decision to trust Christ. Over and over, I have heard them say, "Oh, I know who God is." Great, but what they apparently do not know is the verse in James which says, "You believe that there is one God. You do well. Even the demons believe—and tremble" (James 2:19, NKJV)! The point is, it has to be more than just "believing" that there is a God. Even the demons believe that! The question is, are *you* willing to trust God and devote yourself to following that one and only God for the rest of your life?

That is where I was for years and years. I believed that God existed. I even prayed to God and to Jesus and to Mary and to anybody else who I thought might hear my prayers. But in reality, I was in the same boat as the demons in James chapter 2. I was definitely not saved. I was no closer to a personal relationship with Christ than the man on the moon. I had to eventually come to terms that I was going to hell if I didn't change my ways.

To be saved, we must first confess with our mouth that Jesus Christ is Lord. Say it! This helps to dispel the myth that there is something you can "do" in order to earn your salvation. Say, "Jesus, you are my Lord and I need you to be my Savior. I have nothing or no-body like you in my life. I am confessing to you right now and asking you to become my personal Lord and Savior." Then we must believe in the birth, death, buri-al and the resurrection. We can't trust Christ as Savior if He wasn't born, died, was buried, and then three days later rose again. He did all of that for you and me. Even more so, He did it willingly.

We must realize that Christ doesn't *need* us, rather, He *wants* us. You and I must realize that we are the ones who NEED Jesus. But how can we be saved once we finally realize our *need* to be saved? Again, "For with the <u>heart</u> one believes unto righteousness, and with the <u>mouth</u> confession is made unto salvation" (Romans 10:10, NKJV). You can't have one of these without the other. They both go hand-in-hand. There has to be a time and a place in your life in which you can truly say that you came to believe and trust (at the heart level) that Jesus died for you and that you needed Him in your life.

After that, though, did you have the faith and courage to make a public (out loud) stand for Him? This doesn't mean you had to make a big show of things or have 50 people witness your baptism. But if Christ was merely a passing thought in your head, then you should probably rethink whether you were actually saved in the past or not. So, if you cannot recall a time like this, then please ask yourself if you are really saved? It isn't my place to say that you definitely are *not* saved. However, part of the reason for writing this book was to help people recognize where they stand with God. So, if this book is making you realize that maybe you are not saved, then praise the Lord, I didn't waste yours or my time in writing it! Take a deep breath. Is there still air in your lungs? If so, then you have time right now, to confess with your mouth and believe in your heart and ask Jesus Christ to become your savior this very moment. Congratulations if you just did! Now, keep reading.

Romans 10:13 goes on to tell us, "for whoever calls on the name of the Lord shall be saved" (NKJV). That is great news. By the way, *whoever* means anybody. That means you and me and everybody else in-between. You say, "why do I have to be saved?" Because of the sin in your life. Only saved people go to heaven, and the only way to be saved is through a relationship with Jesus Christ. How can you be saved? By believing with your heart and confessing with your mouth that Jesus is Lord. The Bible is very straight-forward on all of this.

My most prized Bible verse, the one I go to all of the time and treasure in my heart, is John 14:6: "Jesus said to him, 'I am the way, the truth, and the life. No one comes to the Father except through Me'" (NKJV). The bottom line of this verse is that if you and I want to go to heaven, then there has to be a time and a place when and where we have gone through Jesus (i.e. having a relationship with Him). The God of the universe desires to have an intimate relationship with each one of us. It is the only way we can get to heaven. Some will trust in Christ, but most, unfortunately, will not.

When I think about Christ on the cross, my heart is beyond saddened. I am more than glad Christ did what He had to do, but how He did it is truly unfathomable. I think of all of the people who will never trust Christ as Savior. They *know* what Jesus did on the cross, at least many of them do, but knowing is not the same as being converted. It's not the same as submitting to the lordship of Christ and trusting Him as Savior. For so many, the horrific death of Christ on the cross, apparently, is not enough proof of His love for us. Jesus went to the cross and died knowing full-well that the majority of people would never accept Him as the only way to heaven. So, while that is tragic for people who refuse to accept Christ, I am beyond grateful that Jesus gave His life anyway, for the minority, because that minority includes me! He died for all, even though He knew that not everyone would accept Him. That, my friends, truly is *agape* love – the love that only the Father could have towards his children (you and I).

With that in our minds, Christians ought to thank Jesus daily for His unconditional sacrifice on our behalf. At some point many of us realized there was no other way and that we were in a sinful and hopeless situation, but then Jesus made it possible for us to be forgiven and redeemed. That is something to be thankful for! Revelation 3:20 says, "Here I am! I stand at the door and knock. If anyone hears my voice and opens the door, I will come in and eat with that person, and they with me" (NIV). I want you to think about this for a moment. Look down at your chest. Do you see a door handle on the outside of your body leading to your heart? No, right? Do you know why? Because God is simply knocking at the door of your heart and ever so patiently waiting for you to open up the door to let Him in. There is no outside door handle. You are the one who has to sense His knock and hear His call, and then open up the door to your heart and to your life and invite Him in. Once you do that, your life will never be the same. It is a life-altering, mind-blowing, eternal address-changing kind of an experience. No other experience compares to getting saved, because there is nothing else like our God!

The Gospel has been shared diligently with you throughout this book. If you have not already done so, would you please open up the door to your heart and let Jesus Christ come in and eat with you? Get your soul saved right here and right now while you still can.

We are fairly deep in the Gospel sharing right now. Can you honestly answer this question? Are you saved? Can you think of the time when you got saved? Or are you one of those who made a decision when you were really young and now, looking back, you know it was just an emotion at the time and wasn't really a life-changing event? Have you since realized your need of the Savior? The Good News of the Gospel is still available to you. Even now, you have the opportunity to say:

Jesus, please forgive me of my sins. God, I am truly sorry for my wrongdoings. Lord, I repent of my sins right now. Jesus, I believe you came to this earth, went to the cross and died for my sins.

I believe that three days later you arose out of the grave and defeated death. Right now, Jesus, I am confessing to you and asking you to become my Lord and my Savior. Redeem my soul here today. God, save me right now. I pray all of this in the mighty name of our Lord and Savior Jesus Christ. Amen.

Take a deep breath. If you just prayed this, and you wholeheartedly meant it, welcome to the Jesus family. You are now my new brother or sister in Christ. If you are a dude reading this, you're my new brotha from another motha. If you are a woman reading this and you just prayed to received Christ, then now you are my new sista from another mista. I am just having a little fun! I am telling you that there is no greater feeling, especially in today's uncertain world, to know that God is now truly your heavenly Father. You now belong to Him for eternity, you are safe and secure, you are saved from the eternal consequences of your sins, and you, my friends, are heaven-bound when you leave this world.

I have two stories that I would like to share. First, a great cutting horse trainer friend of mine by the name of Phil Sappington, called me one day and said we needed to go see a friend of his who was not doing very well. Now, this man we were going to visit was a good man. He did a lot of beneficial things for the surrounding communities and even for some of the local churches. We went to his house and there he was, laid up in bed, and not in good spirits at all. I really had no idea why I was invited over there, but the Lord was about to reveal it to me.

It turned out that it wasn't my buddy Phil who thought it would be a good idea to visit, but rather the man himself is the one who had requested my visit. So, we made some small conversation and then I asked the man why he wanted me to come see him. He said, "Pastor, I want you to pray for me. I am sick." Ok, I thought, that is plum doable. I pray with people every day. When telling this story before, I have said that I don't know what prompted me to ask this next question, but the truth of the matter is that I absolutely **do** know what prompted me. I simply asked the man one question. I said, "how many years have you been saved?" He was an older man, so I was expecting a big number (not a good assumption on my part, but that is what I was expecting). He said, "when I was twelve years of age, I had a preacher tell me that if I would join his church and be baptized, that I could go to heaven. You just asked me how many years I have been saved, and to tell you the truth, I don't know if I am saved."

And then it became instantaneously clear why God had brought me to this man's bedside. I immediately grabbed his frail hands and asked him if he had ever trusted Christ as his Lord and Savior and asked God to forgive him of his sins? Again, he replied, "I joined a church and got baptized."

This man was not saved. He had done so much good in his lifetime and yet, in his heart, he knew he was not saved. I asked him if he was ready to turn his life over to the Lord Jesus Christ. He looked up with tears in his eyes and said yes. My friend, Phil, was sitting on a chair a few feet away. He moved closer and all three of us grabbed each other's' hands and right there in this man's bedroom, he prayed to receive Christ. It was an amazing, God-ordained visitation. Phil looked at me and said, "I have never witnessed somebody being saved outside of church." I said, "well you have now." Man is God good!

When it is your time to be saved, it really doesn't matter where you are. I wish I could have somehow captured the look on this man's face. It was pure *relief* that had come over him. He was now saved and he knew it. It just never gets old watching people pray to receive Christ. God is so good all of the time.

Secondly, my friend who I have mentioned earlier, Dean Cook, and I went to a McDonald's for breakfast one morning. We got to visiting with one of the ladies who worked there and who had some questions about Christianity. She told us that she *hoped* that she was going to heaven. Well, it was a little busy and it just wasn't the right time to have a true Gospel conversation. We asked her what time she got off and she told us 1 o'clock. We said we would be back then. Sure enough, at 1:00 p.m. we went back to McDonald's and there she was waiting for our return. On a side note, it is very important to always keep your word about things like this. If we would have stood her up, I don't imagine she would have given Christianity much credence ever again. Anyway, we sat in the back of the restaurant and simply shared with her the Gospel. She told us that she had been baptized about four years earlier. She said the preacher had told her that if she would get baptized, then she could be saved. Who is teaching these kinds of things!? That is completely contrary to biblical teachings on salvation. You don't get baptized to be saved; you get saved, by faith, and then you get baptized.

We asked her if she had trusted Christ with her soul and if she had repented of her sins. She said, "no, I got baptized and thought that was all I needed to do." My heart hurts for people like these, who have been led astray by either *fraudulent*, or at the very least,

222

incompetent Christian "teachers."

Actually, I have spoken to countless people over the years who were baptized but were never saved. Children often do it because their parents want them to do it or they experience peer pressure from their friends. Adults often get baptized because they are lied to by preachers and pastors and led to believe that they can be saved by being dunked in some water. But how awful it would be to live your whole life and then die only to find out that you were not saved? You did everything you were "told" to do, but yet you never trusted Christ with your heart. The last words you would ever hear would be God the Father saying, "depart from me, I never knew you."

My friends, there is a way that you can be saved *and* know that you are saved. You can make a conscious decision to follow Jesus for the rest of your days. You just have to want to do it and mean it. The Bible says you must repent (Acts 2:38) and you must have faith (Ephesians 2:8). We have been through all of that. Again, I ask, are you saved? Do you know that you know that you are? It is a question that should make you think. I am at the point in my life and ministry, that I surely don't mind asking such a personal question.

I can't think of one time growing up or even as a younger adult, did somebody ever ask me if I was

FROM RANGE RIDIN' TO SOUL SEEKIN'

saved. I don't know how I might have answered that question back then, but knowing what I know now, I sure do wish that some Christian somewhere would have asked me some tough questions that caused me to begin thinking about eternal things. Nobody cared for me enough to find out if I had a relationship with Jesus? That is a little depressing to think about even now, after all of these years. But I have learned from those days. Let us, you and I, start a new trend. Let us actually care for people's souls. Let us be willing to ask some uncomfortable questions of people. That would be fantastic, wouldn't it? I don't want to *play* church I want to actually *be* the church outside of the four walls of the church building. Now we are talking.

What if when we said, "hey, I will pray for you," we actually meant that we would pray for them right then and there? It shouldn't matter if you are at the post office, gas station, grocery store, rehab, cop shop, school, or just walking down the street. Maybe if we actually looked like a Christian, we wouldn't have to tell people that we are a Christian – there's a thought. How about we start to *live* our faith, and not just *talk* about it. Talking about something and actually doing something are typically two totally different things. I don't want to be known as a talker I want to be known as a doer. Hmmm, that sounds vaguely like some verses out of the Book of James (lol). Maybe if we actually tried to seek out lost souls instead of gossip about them, maybe we would see some differences in our own lives and positive changes in the lives of others.

If you haven't noticed, I genuinely want this book to make each one of us examine ourselves. Who are we? What are we doing with this one life that God has given to us? How can we live differently in order to please the Lord? It is said that *insanity* is doing the same thing over and over expecting a different result. So, let us learn from others (and our own past mistakes), make adjustments in our lives, and become a better and more caring Christian brother or sister. This pleases God. Period.

Now, let me explain one more thing about God. Even after all of that talk about "saving," there's even more! If you have truly received Christ, in addition to the gift of forgiveness and eternal life, you have another gift as well. God gives you the Holy Spirit. I want to share these encouraging words with you from the Gospel of John:

> If you love me, keep my commands. And I will ask the Father, and he will give you another advocate to help you and be with you forever—the Spirit of truth. The world cannot accept him,

because it neither sees him nor knows him. But you know him, for he lives with you and will be in you. I will not leave you as orphans; I will come to you. Before long, the world will not see me anymore, but you will see me. Because I live, you also will live. On that day you will realize that I am in my Father, and you are in me, and I am in you. Whoever has my commands and keeps them is the one who loves me. The one who loves me will be loved by my Father, and I too will love them and show myself to them. (John 14:15-21, NIV)

Wow! An absolutely free gift given to us along with our salvation. Notice it says in verse 16 that He will be with us forever (i.e., He will never leave us). That means you can't put the Holy Spirit on a shelf and leave Him there. He goes with us everywhere we go. That is a great thing especially when we consider some of the practical implications of that.

Let me pick on the men again for a moment. Let's say you have to go out of town on a business trip. You see some places downtown that you know you shouldn't step foot in and you know your wife would be very upset if you did. Let me ask you this question. Are you really going to take the Holy Spirit into that kind of place? Because remember, He's going everywhere you do, because He is never going to leave us (John 14:16). So, we all know the obvious answer is, no, we shouldn't go there. That is exactly what we do, though, if we are saved and yet decide to make those kinds of choices and go to those kinds of places. Who in their right mind would want to take the Holy Spirit somewhere like that? Nobody. You cannot leave Him at the hotel and pick Him back up later. You can't ask Him to wait in your truck or to stay at home. When you are saved, the Holy Spirit dwells in you, forever.

Now maybe somebody reading this book, might say, "Well that's not fair. Where's the fun in that?" Really? Sounds to me like the Holy Spirit just saved you from sinning, or maybe even saved your marriage. That is one of the Holy Spirit's roles – to help guide and direct us in life. He does so much more than just that; it would take another entire book to try and unpack it all. And even then, it wouldn't be enough. Let's just say, if you are saved, then by the grace of God, He has seen fit to in-dwell us through the Holy Spirit. And that is how it will be for the rest of our days here on this earth. Our God is just that generous and good!

No discussion of the Gospel of Jesus Christ would be complete without at least mentioning, maybe, the one verse that best puts the entire Gospel in a nutshell.

John 3:16 says, "For God so loved the world, that he gave his only begotten Son, that whosoever believeth in him should not perish, but have everlasting life (KJV). If you have read this final chapter and for some reason you are still not sure about this Gospel, this one verse sums up what Christ came into the world to do. He loved us, He gave Himself to us, He asks us to believe in Him, and if we will then He will not let us perish (i.e. go to hell for eternity). We can have everlasting life through Him. This is a promise that God gives to us. But each individual has a very important decision to make about whether or not they will trust and follow Jesus Christ.

On January 8, 2009, Tim Tebow was the quarterback for the University of Florida football team and was playing in the National College championship game. In the "eye black" he wore under his eyes, he wrote "John" under one eye and "3:16" under the other eye. During and after the game, it is reported on the Internet that 94 million people conducted an online search of that verse. When Tebow was interviewed, he said this: "Honestly my first thought was how do 94 million people not know John 3:16?" He went on to say how humbled he was to serve a BIG God.

The above story gets even crazier. Fast forward exactly three years later, on January 8, 2012. Tebow was now playing in the NFL for the Denver Broncos. They were in a playoff game against the Pittsburg Steelers. In overtime, Tebow threw an 80-yard pass to win the game. Nothing crazy exciting about that, right? Well here is the breakdown of the statistics from that game. During the game, Tebow threw for 316 yards. His yards per rush were 3.16. His yards per completion were 31.6. The time of possession was 31.6 minutes. Look at what our God did on that particular night. We surely can all agree that this goes well beyond coincidence. In the game, Tebow set an NFL record for yards per completion in a playoff game at 31.6. Even media sources marveled that Tebow's passing yards (316) and yards per completion (31.6) reminded them of that famous Bible verse, John 3:16. Amazingly, the Nielsen TV ratings for the game peaked at 31.6. When asked, Tebow said "A lot of people will say it's a coincidence, but I say BIG GOD." One little Bible verse that went viral all because of one person writing in the black under his eyes, "John 3:16." God can use anything that He wants to bring glory to Himself.

This Bible verse tells us all we need to know about the love of God. God requires a perfect sacrifice, because He is perfect. Makes sense, right? So, any sacrifice that would be offered on the behalf of sinners, would have to be perfect. What did God do? He loved the world enough to give the world an absolute perfect sacrifice – Himself! God, himself, stepped out of heaven, took on human flesh, and dwelt on the earth among humans.

God knew the world would need a way to be able to have everlasting life. So, Jesus became the *propitiation* for our sins. I know I said I wouldn't be using very many big words, but this is one word that we should all know and understand. It just means that Christ's death on the cross was pleasing to God. It reconciled us to God, at least for everyone who would believe. Jesus became the *atonement* for our sins. Jesus did for us what we could not do for ourselves. He lived a perfect and sinless life so that His death would be considered payment (in full) for our sins. No matter how good of a life any of us could live, it still wouldn't be perfect, and so we are unable to offer God "enough" of a sacrifice on our own to solve our sin problem. But God so loved the world that He sent Jesus Christ to solve our sin problem for us. So, "whosoever believeth in Him," will be found righteous enough in God's eyes to live with Him in Heaven for eternity. But again, it isn't because WE were perfect or WE were deserving of everlasting life. It's because of HIM and what HE did on our behalf. That's love.

I can tell you there is mass confusion out there about

what <u>we</u> are able to do to secure our own salvation. But the truth is the only way any of us can become righteous today is by the blood of the Lamb (Jesus Christ). There is no other way. We can't be righteous enough for God by ourselves. Rather, Jesus made it possible for us to be righteous (by receiving HIS righteousness). Again, God did what nobody else could do, He sacrificed His one and only son. The message of John 3:16 is not limited to only a few. It says that "whosoever" believes in Him should not perish, but have everlasting life. Are you a *whosoever*? I am! Will you believe in the One who came to take your place on the cross? I have! Do you believe that someday you can have everlasting life? I do! Each one of us will eventually take our last breath on this earth. Are you ready for that day? I am! If you are not, you had better be getting ready. None of us are promised tomorrow.

How long has it taken you to read this book? A few hours, a few days, a week, or maybe even a month? Do you realize that each day that God has given to you was an absolutely free gift that He did not have to give to any of us? He doesn't want to see anybody perish, but God being the loving God He is, allows us to say *yes* or *no* to Him. For those who have put their faith in Christ, their eternal destination will be heaven above. If you still can't see enough evidence that you need to be saved, and you never repent of your sins and turn to Jesus (and you leave this world that way) then your final destination will be hell. Who in their right mind wants that?

Franklin Graham once reportedly said, "I don't know everything in this Bible, but I believe it all to be true." None of us will ever know the entire Bible flawlessly. But that doesn't mean we can't trust what God has written. The Bible is here for us to learn from, and to follow it as closely as possible in our lives. His Word never changes (praise God!). It is also a moral compass to help us to know right from wrong. A fun acronym for BIBLE is **B**asic **I**nstructions **B**efore **L**eaving **E**arth. Everybody always wants a guide to help get us through life. Well, the Bible not only does that, but also gives us instructions on how to get to the <u>next</u> life! The Bible is right there. You probably already own one (if not more than one). But we have to open it on a regular basis and learn what God would have us to learn from it every single day.

I would like to pray a blessing on each one of you who has taken the time to read and finish this book. You surely noticed that I tried my hardest to include things that would benefit both Christians and non-Christians alike. If you are a Christian already, I pray that it has opened your eyes to some different ways of thinking and evangelizing. If you have not turned your life over to Jesus Christ yet, I pray that you will before it is too late.

The stories I shared throughout this book are all true. No names were changed. These were all real people that God had put in my life. Also, please know that the stories I shared are only a fraction of the stories that God has allowed Rebecca and me to be a part of over the past 10 years. If they were exciting to you, just wait until God allows you the privilege of being a part of what He desires to do in *your* circles of influence. If you will allow Him to work through you, to accomplish His purposes, you will have stories to tell too! I will be just as excited to hear of your adventures in the Lord, as you, hopefully, have enjoyed hearing about mine.

My final thought is this: The ultimate goal in writing this book was to see souls won for Jesus Christ. Rebecca coined a phrase when we first got into the ministry. She would say, "even if it's for only one person." That slogan is true for this book as well. All of the time and effort that have been poured into this book will have all been worth it, if even one person gets saved.

Thank you for taking the time to read. If you have benefited from this book in any way, I would love to hear from you. Also, should you feel led, one of the ways you can support Rebecca's and my ministry is to pray for us (obviously), but also feel free to recommend this book to a family member, friends, or even your whole church. May God bless you as you continue learning about Him and learning new ways to serve Him. You can do this. Now, get after it! To God be the glory!

Reader Reviews

Everyone needs a coach and guide. When one looks at a winning football teams or successful parents they will find a coach or guide behind the success. In Scripture, the list of encouragers includes men and women such as Aaron, Hanna, Nathan, Mordecai and Barnabas. Each of these provided guidance or coaching in matters of faith and practice. Their results gave us Moses, Samuel, David, Esther and Paul.

In *From Range Ridin' to Soul Seekin'* Pastor James Scott provides the encouragement one needs to walk with Jesus. These pages will build your confidence as a Christ follower. If you desire to grow as a disciple, this book is for you.

Dr. Rodney Harrison
President, The Baptist Home of the
Missouri Baptist Convention
Professor of Christian Education,
Midwestern Baptist Theological Seminary

I met James Scott on a horse. From that meeting he invited me to participate in the National High School Rodeo Evangelism ministry. It was there I began to see first-hand the impact that James has on other's lives.

God has taken a pretty good cowboy and repurposed his life for Kingdom work.

I invite you to read his story. You will be inspired and encouraged in your own walk with our Lord Jesus Christ.

Don Lum
Director of Evangelism
Mississippi Baptist Convention Board

James has written a very helpful book that will inspire many to share their faith in Jesus Christ with others. For some Christians, articulating their faith is intimidating and sometimes overwhelming. "Range Ridin' to Soul Seekin'" gives you practical steps and a simple strategy to become a soul winner and kingdom builder. As Scott says in his book, 'Sharing is our responsibility; saving is God's.'

I also appreciate the emphasis the Wyoming cowboy evangelist places on the importance of mentoring believers after they come to Christ. That, after all, is a very important part of the mandate of the Great Commission.

Jim Burnett
Pastor and Christian Western Author

"What if God were to take a plain-spoken cowboy and make a preacher out of him? What if God were to move that preacher from the ranch to the mission field? What if God were to give that man a passion for rounding up souls? That is what God did when he saved and called James Scott. With all the cowboy traits—raw obedience, weathered determination, and focused passion—James Scott is a Cowboy Preacher. While this book tells a story of God's redemption and calling, James lays out in simple terms his ministry philosophy and evangelistic methodology. His ability to communicate complex theological principles in the simplest terms is appealing and refreshing. Moreover, it reveals what I have always known about my friend; he is more than a Cowboy preacher; he is a Cowboy theologian."

Dr. Brett Golson

Thank You's

I would like to publicly give thanks to the Lord Jesus Christ for giving me the experiences to write about and the energy to see this book to fruition. It is by His saving grace that I am who I am today. His call on my life to be a soul-winner is what drives me, and He is always faithful to put me in contact with the right people at the right time. All glory, honor, and praise go to Him!

I would also like to thank my very best friend in the world, Reverend Mark Dickson. God put Mark in my life when I was a young Christian man. I needed what Mark had, and Mark wanted what I had—he wanted to be a cowboy. He mentored me and taught me how to live for Christ. We have stayed in close contact, now, for nearly 16 years. When I felt that God was calling me into the ministry, Mark was the first person I contacted. After sharing with him what I felt God was leading me to do, he put a name to it: pioneering ministry. He told me it would be very difficult, but that he would be praying for me. He offered to do anything in his power to help me succeed. He has always been my listening ear. He has helped me in my ministry life more than any other man. That is saying a lot, because God has put some incredible men in my path. Mark, I will always cherish our friendship and will love you as deeply as a Christian brother can love. Thank you for believing in me and pushing me when I needed to be pushed.

A great big thank you to another one of my friends, Dr. Shane Stone. Shane, you inspired me to keep writing and to see this book project through to the very end. I appreciate the tips and advice you offered. Any time I was stuck or looking for a different way to say something, you always came through for me. Thank you for all of your help in the editing process. People should know that Dr. Stone has also written a book titled, "Preach Better Sermons." Feel free to check it out at Amazon, Barnesandnoble, Booksamillion, or Christianbook.com.

Finally, I want to say thank you to my wife, Rebecca. She has been by my side for over 26 years now. She has inspired me to be a better husband, father and pastor. Her intuition has helped me more times than I can count. She is my number-one fan, but she is also brutally honest with me. Everyone needs a spouse like that! I know she has prayed for me to be a godly husband and father, and I have tried my very best, with God's help, to be the answer to her prayers. Together, we raised three wonderful boys, who are now all men. Her sense of adventure and her love for the Lord make me fall in love with her again and again every single day. Rebecca Scott, I love you more than words and across borders. May God continue to have His hand on your life, our marriage, and our ministry, till death do we part!

Contact the Author

If you enjoyed reading this book, and you would like to arrange for the author, James Scott, to speak at your church or your next function, please reach out to him via email at hccjamess@yahoo.com. Pastor James also encourages any feedback you are willing to provide. He would love to hear your questions, comments, stories, or encouraging words. If you prayed to receive Christ as your Lord and Savior while reading this book, or if you used this book to help minister to someone in your circle, please email that information as well. To God be the glory!

https://outskirtspress.com/pastorjamesscott

CPSIA information can be obtained
at www.ICGtesting.com
Printed in the USA
JSHW010135040922
29963JS00002B/12

9 781977 233615